GLORY DAZE

GLORY DAZE

Chris M.

authorHOUSE

AuthorHouse™
1663 Liberty Drive
Bloomington, IN 47403
www.authorhouse.com
Phone: 1 (800) 839-8640

© 2015 Chris M. All rights reserved.

No part of this book may be reproduced, stored in a retrieval system, or transmitted by any means without the written permission of the author.

Published by AuthorHouse 08/21/2015

ISBN: 978-1-5049-2502-0 (sc)
ISBN: 978-1-5049-2501-3 (e)

Print information available on the last page.

Any people depicted in stock imagery provided by Thinkstock are models, and such images are being used for illustrative purposes only.
Certain stock imagery © Thinkstock.

This book is printed on acid-free paper.

Because of the dynamic nature of the Internet, any web addresses or links contained in this book may have changed since publication and may no longer be valid. The views expressed in this work are solely those of the author and do not necessarily reflect the views of the publisher, and the publisher hereby disclaims any responsibility for them.

Contents

Foreword..vii

Chapter 1   "Schools Out"..1

Chapter 2   "Same fields but evening.. 1967 first year of
            Little League" 24

Chapter 3   Wild, wild …Baseball memories- 1968..................31

Chapter 4   Summer of 69…memories- Season 3....................42

Chapter 5   School and the last year of little league"................58

Chapter 6   After Little League- the following two years...........67

Chapter 7   2nd year of Pony League for the Cardinals.................80

Chapter 8   The last year of Pony League....................................84

Foreword

I have thought of writing this story for some time. Now I drive thru my old hometown of Gas City, In and see how things have changed over the past 50 years. On the south side of town once stood the old sandlot diamonds at the corner of 7th and "D" street. The ball fields of old have now been replaced with houses. Most people living there now know nothing of the nightly glow of the ball field lights on Tuesday and Thursday nights throughout the summer. They are oblivious to the roars which would erupt when a homerun was hit or when a particular team won in thrilling fashion. This is a story of growing up in a small town on a dust blown set of fields called sandlots. I know little of the legends that came and played before me except like dinosaurs they existed. Now I look in the mirror and see something which reminds me of a something from the Jurassic period as well. Just like all the great ball players of old. Eventually time raises up new and even better heroes to play the wonderful game of baseball. The same is true even on the microcosmic scale of a small town. So I hope this book serves as a time machine back to a very different and distinct age. This book looks back at a time when life seemed simpler. Those of us who played gathered by day to play a game we loved. Many came back to play in the organized leagues which played into the night. I was working at a site in Az and watched dust devils spin in clouds of dust. I even remember seeing one on the Little League field I will discuss. I remember thinking how time seemed to pick up and take away those fields that produced a lifetime of memories for so many.

The sandlot life by day was the only form of baseball many ever played. Others like myself also played little league and pony league and beyond. From the bad bounces of the hot summer days, life on a sandlot was coarse and brutal at times. It was the melting pot where young boys from age 7 through even 15 and even older gathered to play an "unorganized" form of baseball. There were no video games in that day, the first video game Pong was a few years away. In fact, TV was the latest technological breakthrough. It was a time of riding bikes-sting rays with banana seats and baseball cards clicking away in the spokes. It was a time of ball gloves draped on the handle bars. Many times the bike riders carried a passenger or even two one on the handle bars and possibly one behind on the back of the seat. Like ants gathering at a picnic somehow players materialized to test and hone their skills. It is a fact that this time passed like dust blowing in the wind. You couldn't tell at the time, but slowly and surely this life was trickling away. It might have simply changed from having fewer kids around. Now you think back and it's all nothing but faded memories. Hundreds of fun morning and afternoon games washed away with time. I'd like to think that maybe somehow though it still lives somewhere or maybe even may live again and if not then at least I hope to capture a part of it in these pages.

Beyond what happened on the ball field this story also chronicles what life was like in the mid 60s to early 70s in this small town built around a river. Surrounding schools called us the "river rats". We were a somewhat scrappy bunch. We were the sons and daughters of those who worked in the nearby factories and made their homes in those small towns. It is an odd river that flows north instead of south like most. Our Mississinewa school mascot was an Indian based on those that had previously lived in the area hundreds of years before. The anecdotes and stories featured in this book may be of interest to those who lived thru the late 60s and early 70s. It may also interest those who just wondered what life might have been like for their father's or grandfathers. I am reasonably sure similar ball playing was going on across the country. Some may read and compare and contrast it to their own experiences in other areas at that time. I am well into my 50s now. Most of what follows comes directly from my own memory(as accurate or inaccurate as that might be). I had a few clippings and kept a few notes. Real names are not used. I am pretty sure the majority of those who grew up and played daily on those sandlots would love to go back and play one more time. Although I like the thought of building a time machine so far though I have not been successful. Maybe it was another case of a few small fish in a small pond. I have known enough fishermen in my time to know that the fish in the stories seemed larger than life. We were all minnows then but even so in both little league and the sandlots in those days there were giants. These giants were legends that everyone who played still remembers. It is still fodder for discussing when we get together to recount their tales of when we were players there.

The book also talks about other things we did for fun in those summers. Some mention of my own school life is also made. Parents, coaches, and teachers all contributed to making these times special for all of us kids that grew up in Gas City.

This is dedicated to all the kids who played there. A special dedication to all those who grew up on or near "C" St and played on the sandlots. I am sad to say a few of our friends and teammates have passed on – like the diamonds we played on soon enough we all will leave this world. If this brings a smile or a chuckle then I guess it has been worth the effort to write. Also this is in large part dedicated to all the parents who in so many ways sacrificed and supported us. In doing so they gave us our opportunity to live this life as youngsters. Finally to the artist who did the sketches in this book, a big thanks to Harold. These times were our glory days.

Chapter 1

"Schools Out"

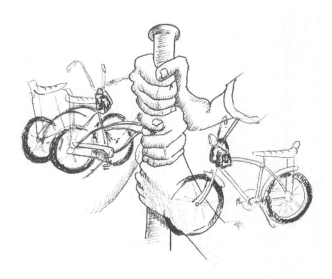

A lot was going on in June of 1967. The world was changing. WWII and the more recent Korean conflict were in the rearview mirror. So I guess it is good that some wars at least stopped. Others were trying to start. Drums of war were also beating in the Middle East marking the 6 day war. Israel miraculously defeated Syria in the Golan Heights and Egypt acquiring many new territories. Although these wars were on other lands they were being brought here to within each household. In those days, instead of the news primarily coming from the newspaper it was being piped directly into the home and in fact into the minds of most US citizens. A generation that grew up with radio was now the first to experience television. With eyes and ears tuned to the nightly news with Walter Cronkite households would be flooded by more of war's bloody reports from Vietnam. Many of our youth were coming home in a body bag. It didn't matter much if you were from New York City or small burg in the middle of the south. Death found too many of our youth. Even so if you didn't have a TV you were likely shopping for one. In the prior years news was just a black and white newspaper article or maybe a distant voice on the static filled radio. Although I have seen shows that mention during WWII some news on the war came by way of the big screen on the movie theatres. As most wars differ from their predecessor Vietnam was a war very different from WWII. In fact, a great general once said every war is not quite like the one that preceded it. This one was fought in the jungles. It was an ugly hit and run "guerilla war". These years included a mandatory draft and registering for the draft. It was a time when burning your draft card was a proud day for some. Even as a kid I sort of figured that I might end up trudging thru rice patties looking for an enemy who basically came and went like a ghost. It's funny how your perceptions start to form at a young age. Vietnam is actually a lush green and beautiful place. I have been blessed to have had a couple friends from Vietnam over the years. Both were "boat people" who braved incredible odds to escape following the communist takeover in Vietnam. However, rice patties were not going to be my fate. The draft had ended shortly before I even had to register. I do remember breathing a sigh of relief. If this wasn't enough war, the cold war was well under way with the then Soviet Union. Communism and fear of communism was spreading across Asia.

Wars and rumors of wars were fortunately not the only topic of nightly news. Let's discuss technology of the time. Arthur C Clark's 3rd Law states that "Any sufficiently advanced technology is indistinguishable from magic." The same magic(new technology)of the television was also bringing reports on the dawning of another breaking technology-the space program. In that time as the baby boomers(1946-1964)we were the generation that had shall we say boomed- Clark couldn't have been more accurate about that magical time. We were the first generation to grow up with the television. We were the first generation to see the orbits of Gemini, the moon trips of Apollo and then to see the Space shuttles and planetary exploration. The German's had attacked England with the V2 rocket in the 40s. The "greatest generation" may have just beat them in the nick of time. The United States had put some of the German scientists like Werner Von Braun to work on our space program. My parents grew up with radio and programs like "War of the Worlds", "The Shadow", and "The Lone Ranger". The industrial age and the automobile marked a big territory in this time. Ours would be the first generation raised on and in many cases by the television. Our generation would also see "the final frontier"…. space begin to be explored. The Russians had taken the lead with the launch of small sputnik satellite. A great memory just was around the corner when the television brought us the moon landing on July 20, 1969. On that day when Armstrong set foot on the Moon he said "One small step for man, one giant step for mankind." The US flag was planted. Behind the vision of JF Kennedy we had taken the lead. But there was a dark side to the race. Even in "Wizard of Oz" there were good and bad witches. Both sides had let a genie out of the bottle that could not be put back in. Of course I am referring to the atomic bomb. Suspicion of each other was growing daily in what was defined as the "Cold war". It was more passively referred to as the space race. But it was a scary time. Scary in large part due to images we were watching.

The early TVs were black and white with one or two knobs often connected to an outdoor aluminum mast and VHF/UHF antenna. Some were equipped with an adjustable smaller set of rabbit ears for VHF reception. It was not uncommon for the position of the viewers in the room to affect the signal enough it could be tuned or usually unturned. TVs were heavy and vacuum tube filled. The "electronics" were enclosed in a wooden cabinet. But transistors were coming soon enough though. Plastic and molded cabinets were also coming soon. Folks didn't mind getting up to switch a channel in those days. There were no remote controls to be had. Later while working in Fort Wayne, I was privileged to have had a couple meetings in the Philo Farnsworth commemorative meeting room. Some credit him as being the father of the TV. RCA's visionary leader Sarnoff sought to expand markets for TV as he had with radio. His visions did not include Farnsworth. Bitter court cases marked the years before. Electronics and namely the transistor had burst upon the scene and were working their way into many devices. TVs would soon evolve from black and white to color. Even so the snowy images still were effective in providing all the information and entertainment required in the 60s. There weren't many channels –even if you were in a "good" area you probably didn't get more than 3 or 4 channels. The 3 major networks were about it. By today's standards the screens were small maybe 19" as measured diagonally. There weren't any flat screens in those days. No satellites and therefore no satellite TV.

On the west coast and more specifically the San Francisco area folks were experiencing something quite different. The hippie and drug cultures were growing by number. It was coined the "Summer of Love". Music it seemed had literally transformed overnight. "Rock and Roll" was born right alongside a good majority of the "boomer generation". The funny thing in 1967 the top song was "To Sir with Love" by Lulu. That was hardly a classic rock song as most would define it today. England was quick to adopt the music and then send their repackaged version back to the US in what was known as the "British Invasion". Nothing would ever rival the Beatles and The Rolling Stones or the "King…Elvis". But history shows there was also Chad and Jeremy, the Hollies, the Kinks, the Who and many, many others. With the exception of Elvis most all of these would be called "classic rock" bands. Even those judged as way…way… "way out there" are now classics. Concerts were moving to large outdoor venues. Music was finding its way into about everything and its technology was also changing. Regardless, whoever was popular they likely made an appearance on Sunday evening Ed Sullivan show. I still enjoy watching some of those old episodes with the Stones, the Beatles, the Animals and others. Speaking of Sunday evening TV -Walt Disney had his famous show. Disney land opened smack dab in the middle of the "boomer generation". Disney World in Florida was only 4 years off. Going to Disney was on every kids bucket list.

Parents didn't know how to view the new rock bands. Most judged by the length of their hair. A few including my parents semi-approved list included Elvis, Jerry Lee Lewis, and of course Johnny Cash. People could buy recordings of their favorites on 45 or 33 vinyl records. Audio was also an industry experiencing rapid growth. We all remember the RCA dog listening to a phonograph. If I am not mistaken that played in conjunction with the Disney show. I remember my first 45 was the Beatles "I Wanna hold Your Hand". In those days, I didn't really have enough money to buy the albums(33). I did have a small transistor radio which picked up a couple AM stations though. Later I got a small radio/record player combo unit. You could stack up to 4 records which would play in sequence. That's a far cry from today's iTune technology that can store and play Gigabytes of music from everything from your phone to a lap top computer or mp3 player of some make/model. If a record got scratched there wasn't a lot you could do for it but buy another. Even today, a lot of folks like the sound that comes from the old records-played on the older stereo sets.

This was truly the time of the classics. Today whole channels are devoted to music from this time- that includes satellite radio! My generation would witness the audio revolution; the cassette, the 8 track, the CD, and the MP3. We would see VHS tapes, Beta tapes, and Laser Video disks come and go. Phones were attached to the wall and had rotary dial. No cordless phones then. No cell phones in that day. Like so many of these technologies maybe that is me ..a "classic" as opposed to the fossil/dinosaur my kids think I am. A few of these bands are still drawing thousands and have sold billions of dollars of recordings to a number of generations.

I have mentioned some about the music explosion. In addition, I mentioned Ed Sullivan and Disney. However, I want to shift gears and mention a few other tv shows that were popular. The top shows were on CBS. Surely, this time was the "golden Age" of TV. Beverly Hillbillies and "The Honeymooners" were popular. Others of that era included "Andy Griffin"," Gomer Pyle USMC", "The Lucy Show", "Gunsmoke", and "Family Affair". Coming soon would be the next wave featuring "Gilligan's Island", "I Dream of Jeannie", "The Munsters", and "The Adams Family". I still say the answer to the age old question "Ginger or MaryAnn?" was Jeannie. Now in Fort Wayne many of these shows can still be seen on what they call "antenna tv". With satellite based tv and cable dominating the markets funny that now transmitting the signals by air is a nostalgic thing. Although now they are digital instead of analog signals.

Let's not forget the Saturday morning cartoons. The 3 Stooges, Bugs Bunny, Donald Duck were the Saturday choices. Bullwinkle and Rocky was on Sunday. Adventure series like "Time Tunnel" and "Voyage Under the Sea" would come along. Then one day it got even better. The greatest show ever- at least then… "Lost in Space" was in full swing. The big screen had been around for several years. That year "Jungle Book" was the big movie. Regardless, summer was upon us and that meant no school. In those day's I didn't realize how fast the time would fly by. I know generally everyone was glad when school was out- but probably none more than me. You see I wasn't the ideal student. The ironic thing would be that I would go on and get a 2 yr Electronic Engineering Technology degree, 4 yr Bachelor of Science Electrical Engineering, and even later a Master's in Management. I know some of my teacher's might say- I never would have seen that coming.

My first couple years of school were to put it mildly…rough. We walked to school which was about 5 blocks as opposed to the two miles a lot of the previous generation usually claimed. I guess therefore I had it easy. I remember kicking rocks and throwing them on the way to school. Too bad those skills never really helped much later in life. Even before baseball I had a knack of throwing and throwing pretty accurately. Crabapples in addition to rocks were typical choices. Pears sometimes were thrown too. It seems like there were a lot of rocks lying around that needed thrown in those days.

Recess was the best part of first grade. There was one recess in the morning then lunch and another in the afternoon. In my view it would have been better if all day was recess with a couple 15 minute breaks for class. We played kickball with these pink dimpled rubber balls. It was a game a lot like baseball! A person "rolled the ball" to the kicker. The person kicking would then attempt to kick a fair ball. Those playing defense could catch it in the air and the kicker was out. Runners who were not on a base could be hit or tagged with the ball for an out. Nobody covered a base to catch a thrown ball for the most part. Well come on..it was much more fun to hit the runner with the ball. But I guess a force out was possible. So as with baseball there were bases. One time someone kicked one over the short white fence surrounding the playground and off school property. I hopped the fence went and got it. The teacher in charge(as fate would have it was my 1st grade teacher) started yelling at me when I came back. I thought I had done a good thing. Well, I threw the ball and hit her in the head. So I was introduced to my first of many paddlings. Yes some people these days may find that shocking. I guess school systems weren't up to speed on Dr Benjamin Spock's recommendations not to spank yet. If I would have known that at the time I might have mentioned it to the spanker. You don't hear about kids getting spanked at school now. In my defense, to me those were the streets I walked to/from school on. I looked both ways. Plus nobody had told me any different. I rest my case.

Also during recess I would win dozens of marbles almost every day- in a game we played at recess. Over the first couple years of school

I accumulated a large bucket full of marbles. Many marbles were made of glass and had names such as : "cats eyes"," clearies". Some rarer ones were made of steel and aptly called "steelies". They came in several sizes. Some were large others small. I remember I liked these deep maroon colored translucent ones which I had won. The game involved being able to throw and hit the opponent's marble before he hit yours. There was some strategy involved there. But when in range you had to hit it or you likely lost. The playground area was made of a light colored finely crushed stone..some places almost like sand. I know I got in a couple fights over marbles. That is probably why kids that came after did not know this game it may have been banned. I remember one time as a first grader I won a third graders larger "steelie". That was the most prized and wonderful in most marble players book anyway. He decided not to allow me to have it after I won it fair and square. A brief scuffle ensued. Both of us were taken to the principal. The spelling of the name principal seemed odd in itself. It includes the letters 'p..a..l'. In most of my encounters the principal was not my pal. To my surprise this time he was! The 3rd grader told the truth that I had won it and that he didn't want me to have it. I was allowed to return to class with the marble and he got a whack. Of course I never played that marble again. I am not sure I understood the principal's decision fully. It was, however, my first lesson in justice I guess. I am pretty sure I threw the first punch. That marked my first of many visits with the principal. In the other meetings I found myself at the wrong end of his paddle.

Even in those days it seemed like I was always throwing something. This was the normal past time when walking to and from school. Rocks were the projectile of choice. Nothing really beat the dull clank of connecting with the stop sign at the corner. Over the years the octagon shaped street sign at 7th and "C" recorded some of the better hits which served as badges of honor. The pock marked dents increased over the years, that is for sure, I am not sure it rivaled the surface of the moon but it reminded me of that. Each day the trip to and from school was the best part outside of recess. Once at school, I was forced into a different sort of world. My grades weren't so good. I would simply not do phonics and mostly drew pictures during phonics time. You may ask why not phonics? I can't really give a good answer. I could already read. I could recognize words if I heard someone say them. I know and remember that I drew a lot of pictures. I drew superheros and also characters I saw on cartoons. Also a major theme was dinosaurs. I know the picture of dinosaurs eating my teacher didn't go over too well- At least not with her. I might have been a little less unruly in 2nd but I think I had firmly solidified my grasp on the whacks lead in our school. Things changed in 3rd grade -I had a teacher that sort of kept me in line and my grades were good. She appealed to my interest in science and more specifically chemistry and physics. I was allowed to go to the high school chemistry and physics classes her son taught at the high school. It was a scary land of "giants". In fact, there was a show on TV in those days called "Land of the Giants". When I went to the high school a lot of time I knew the answer but kept quiet when I sensed some of the boys didn't appreciate me being there let alone answering a question. One time one of the boys said if I answer any more questions he was going to set me on the water fountain. That didn't seem like a good place to end up. I remember leaving my last time and thinking at least I didn't get sat on the water fountain. I had kinda learned about some basics of chemistry mostly from my Chemistry sets. I also knew about different reactions. I was even learning some of the math involved and exponential number systems. But I liked physics more. I liked "modern" physics. I knew about Einstein's $E=mc^2$ equations. I knew it was involved in the atomic bomb. By the way in those days a couple times a year along side of fire and tornado drills many school's also had atomic bomb drills. The bank was the only place in town that had the special symbol as a safe place in event of a nuke. Of course not sure why one would hit such a little town- if it did nothing would matter anyway. Glass bottling companies I doubt were at the strategic top of Russian hit list. Nevertheless at school we did drills and crouched under a desk or in the hallway. Don't think it would have helped much.

Another factor in me starting to try and pay attention in school had its roots in the summer. During the summers after first and second grade I had a tutor. At first I wasn't too fond of this plan. Now I look back and realize I also owe a lot to the tutor who found the key to getting me to do the work. The secret she discovered was not so complicated or technical. Instead she provided these wonderful molasses cookies which I would get after doing my work. I think I still remember the wonderful aroma of these. Usually they were in the oven while I was doing the homework. I would get right to work. They were best fresh out of the oven. She was I believe a retired teacher who lived a couple blocks away. Toward the end I was getting the work done in half the time. Usually it resulted in an extra cookie or two. The method worked. I wasn't meaning to get real autobiographical in this book. I hope together these parts help paint a picture of how I was and how life for an elementary student was. Cookies are still about my favorite thing today. I still periodically buy molasses ones. I hope I have given enough background it takes some of you back. Younger readers I hope you can sort of start to form a picture of life then. Life was pretty localized back then. I couldn't have imagined the world of sports which had already seen giants come and go. I certainly knew nothing of the world of baseball. Baseball had seen the likes of Babe Ruth, Lou Gehrig, Ty Cobb, Mickey Mantle, and Jackie Robinson. I didn't know or didn't care…yet. I certainly was unaware that was about to radically change. It would never really leave me as I would participate in some form of ball for decades to come.

By discussing TV and school I have digressed a bit –Let's get back to important stuff. Back to the summer and school being out. It would be years later Alice Cooper would come out with the song "Schools Out", however if I had a theme song in those days that that had to be it. I barely made it to second grade. Turbulent times have always been used to describe the 60s. The 60s were indeed a time of great change. My life was about to make a dramatic change. It all started one late May or early June morning with a bing bong…and a knock at the door.

Then came another and another... bing-bong. It sounded urgent. Looking back I wonder what if I had not answered it. I am not sure how life would have been, knowing now I would have thousands of hours hours of fun playing some form of ball for the next 38 years or so. I doubt I would have played as much or even as well had I not also played sandlot ball. So, I guess in reality it was urgent. Rarely, did anyone come to the door let alone at about 730 AM. It was my grade school friend John. He said everyone was getting together on the corner for a ball game. I didn't know who "everyone" was but I knew I wanted to play. My mind flashed back to a week or so before and remembering riding in the car bouncing over the railroad tracks with my dad. Our destination was the high school gym. He had mentioned the little league draft was coming up a couple weeks earlier. At that time, I remember being tentative about playing but decided to try it. So the draft had taken place and maybe even an organized practice or two. I am not sure of the position the Yanks drafted from but I was the first pick drafted by a local legendary power hitter for the local Owens-Illinois industrial team. Work baseball teams what a great concept! My team was the Yankees. The Yankees wore black T-shirts which I think had the team name on front and said something on back about the 3 way recreation league which sponsored all teams. The leagues were comprised of the American league and the National League. As best I remember the team names and colors are shown below:

AL	NL
Yankees (Black)	Cardinals(Orange)
Senators (Maroon)	Phillies(Maroon)
Pirates (Green)	Mets(Black)
Tigers (grey or yellow	Giants(Yellow)
Orioles (Orange)	Red Sox(Red)
White Sox(Royal Blue)	Astros(Purple)
Dodgers (Purple)	A's(?)
Cubs (Navy blue)	Braves(Grey?)

Not all kids had real baseball pants but my parents bought me some. I also had hard rubber cleats. I only wore the uniform and cleats for the official Little League games and not out to the sandlot. At that point I was simply a rookie. I knew nothing of the game or certainly not of the local legends that had come before. If I had an older brother I might have saw some of those games.

Noticing John had his bike I grabbed my ball cap, glove, and bat. I had a silver sting ray with banana seat. No "sissie" bar. I threw my glove over the handle bars as I noted he had done. I don't even remember eating. Out the door we went and so it had begun.

We lived in a small three bed room ranch that was at least partially built by my dad. Gas City was divided into a grid. On each side of Main Street the streets were named alphabetically for example "A", "B", "C" and so on. The streets which ran north and south were numbered "1st", "2nd", "3rd" ect. 1st was close to the rail road track. John lived several blocks away I think maybe around "2nd" and "B". Because we were on the south side of Main Street my address would be East South "C". The house would have a number reflecting the N/S road ie 7xx. In fact, in those days I did not know where exactly John lived. But it wasn't far from my grandmother which was a few blocks down "C" St. I am pretty sure I had walked to my grandparents once or twice even at that age. A kid walking several blocks was not too unusual. In those days kids were perfectly safe to walk or ride bikes freely through the town. I guess there wasn't as much crime at least in terms of things parents have to worry about today. Many parents worked in factories in neighboring town or locally in one of the two glass companies. One in fact was a block away from my grandparents and my mother and mom and several relatives worked there.

With parents working early there wasn't a lot of traffic during the days. We quickly navigated the two blocks to the ball field. For me the field was only a couple blocks away-one block to the west and one to the south. It was situated on the south east side of town. The "corner field" as we(I) called it had little more than a small fence back stop. It may have been a section of aluminum fencing that was about 6 feet wide and maybe another 8 feet tall. To call it a back stop was taking some degree of liberty. The fence had curled up at the bottom and balls thrown by all pitchers had a mystical way of finding an open path under the fence. Grass-less spots typically marked the base areas(roughly 60 feet apart). So I guess technically this practice field was not really a sandlot. Sometimes someone would throw down a piece of cardboard to act as the base. There was no pitching rubber on that field. That morning I remember the grass was wet with dew. I was wearing a pair of sneakers which would soon get wet. As the sun rose the grass glistened with a magical glow. Grass seemed greener in those days. It didn't take long for the dew to disappear and the game would begin. It seemed like every day was sunny then. The skies were blue..much bluer than today. There might even had been a lonely cloud or two. The outfield of the corner field butted up against the real little league fence in centerfield. Across 7th street to the east was a large soybean or corn field(depended on the year). Foul balls would find their way into that field and often vanish. A few hundred feet into the soybean field loomed the new huge water tower with the name Gas City painted on the side. In later years "kids" would climb it and paint some graffiti on it. Even to me then(and you know something of my history)that seemed like a bad idea. I am reasonably sure it was there at that time. In fact, there it remains to this date. There are no beans in the field there are only houses. If you go to that corner the water tower doesn't look near as far as I remember it. Many years later another similar water tower somewhat like it was built near the interstate on the exit which goes to town. There was also an older water tower just off of Main Street a couple blocks from city hall. But, I digress.

Concerning chasing fouls in the bean field, if it was an older guy's baseball – you'd better find it…and find it fast. A new white ball was a rare luxury. They usually turned a brownish green in short order. That color didn't distinguish it much from the soybeans. One time, I remember running out into the field to get a foul ball and falling.

My head went straight through a spider web. I rose up and there dangling from my ball cap was a large black and yellow garden spider. I mean large! With this unwelcome guest inches from my face - I had that hat off quicker than …well you could say than jumping jack flash. I shook it off and grabbed the ball and ran back throwing it to the pitcher. I certainly didn't want them to think I was afraid of spiders. I was totally creeped out the next ten minutes at least. Kept my fingers crossed that another ball didn't go into those beans. I had learned a disadvantage of playing left field. To the west of the corner field was a dirt road which ran up to the real field and served as the unreachable "fence" in right field. I think cars could circle the fenced Little League field and get back onto 7th St. In the following years crushed stone was added to the drive. I am sure a rare few balls had to find their way to that driveway. None really come to mind. In fact, usually right field was "closed".

After playing catch for a few minutes and waiting on a few more late arrivals it was time for the game to begin. We all had parked our bikes along "D" street. A popup in that area was like walking a mine field. Not a good idea to knock any bikes that had kickstands over. That was usually a pitcher's problem once in a while. Many times there would be a dozen or so bikes lining the street. Usually the first group would play till around 11 or 12 then that group would break up for lunch. Sure …others would usually show up as the game went on. Captains would graft them in according to whose pick it was- thus that created another risk of being the team with the extra player when someone good shows up late. But the flip side of that I guess there was equal risk the person showing might not be very good either. It dawned on me years later captains may have been aware a certain guy would come later. No problem man. But for now let's discuss the typical start.

That day when we pulled up only a couple others were at the corner field. John's brother and a couple of his friends were waiting. They were a couple years older than John and I. In fact, most all that came in those days were older than me. The exception might have been Jimmy who was only about 6 then I think. Everyone dropped their bats near the edge of the backstop out of the path to first base alongside the row of bikes. Over the next few minutes to half hour a few more showed up. The rules of the sandlots went a lot like this >the two oldest/biggest guys usually were "captains" and chose their own teams in alternating draft fashion. Most times it started with tossing a bat with the handle side up. That would be the case if more than 8 were there.

The bat was tossed and caught at a chosen spot midway on the bat. Then each captain walked his hand strategically toward to the end of the bat on placing his hand above the opposing captain's hand until one of the two could use his thumb of his top hand to of cover the middle of the handle of the bat. That captain then won first pick. Of course during the process you could also choose to not use the full hand but go between using any number of fingers to make it more interesting. So as the new chubby kid I went toward the bottom or maybe even the last pick for a while. Older guys dominated the early rounds of the drafts. Sometimes toward the end of the draft a captain would say OK I'll take "so and so" and you can have the last two. Many times teams had an unequal numbers of players. Usually the one who got the two..got the short end of the stick. Two "out makers" as they(we) were called then. I guess that was me ...an "out maker".

Special rules were in effect for those games. First, usually you didn't have enough people for every position. You almost never had a right fielder or a catcher. Many times in that first year there were less than 8 kids. The back stop was usually the catcher. That meant the pitcher had to cover home on base hits and such. As I mentioned right field was "closed" from the left field foul pole(of the real diamond) then to the imaginary first base line("D" St) – so hitting it in that zone was an automatic out period and vise versa for left handers left field would be closed to from a certain fence post to the imaginary third base line. Nobody appreciated the outfield shifting process required when lefties came to the plate. Balls fielded by the shortstop(many times there was no 3B or 2B) were subject to what was called "pitcher's hand". That meant fielders just threw the ball to the pitcher before the runner crossed the bare spot known as first base for the out. Pitcher's could throw curves and knuckleballs but not fast balls. Pitcher's also served as umpires. Hmm don't remember many arguments though. We had no batting helmets many had no ball caps..rarely did anyone wear sunglasses either. I was reminded at least in my latter sandlot days I had a pair of the flip-up style sunglasses similar to those major leaguers use. Very Joe Coolish I must say.... A few wore shorts. I remember a lot had long pants although sliding didn't happen a lot.

After these pre game activities took place the game would finally start. Since 7th street was used by semitrailers to deliver stuff to the local glass company across town it was not unusual for the pitcher to pause while the truck got through the stop sign. Perfect timing would allow the truck to get by and be 60-80 feet or so down the road. It was a highlight if someone pulled it foul and right off the side or back of the trailer. A few times that happened. Typically there would be 3 maybe 4 bats to pick from. Often times they were bigger than an 8/9 year old could effectively use- I mean even 33" or 34" were common. These length's were beyond that allowed in little league(32"). Of course we all learned to "choke up". Another thing you quickly learned is avoid using an older guys bat- cause if you crack it - it meant trouble. Thus everyone knew how the trademark needs to be up/down not facing the pitcher as the bat crosses the plate. So some basic skills began to form on those fields at that time. The older guys could hit the ball a lot farther and harder for that matter. So this ritual went on daily whenever the sun shown and rain stayed away. Typically we played from 8-1130 AM then most days some number of that group reconvened around 1. I am pretty sure by 330 or 4 you were done and heading home.

Of course..on Tue and Thur if you were in little league your games would start maybe around 5 till 9 at the real diamond. In the empty field to the south of the little league diamond was an old abandoned semitrailer or some metal trailer. In later years a concession stand was added behind the main LL diamond. To the west of the little league diamond was the old Pony League field. It was much larger. Pony league ages ran from age 13 to 15. The next level you might say. The drive near the field was covered with black colored cinder flakes. Wrecking your bike there would result in many cuts from the flakes. These I believe originated from some part of the glass making process nearby Owens-Illinois. That field had once seen the likes of Ted Williams and Johnny Pesky who played for nearby air force base. For the record, there was another LL diamond in Jonesboro across the river at their park. That ball field still remains to this date. Another was also built next to it. For half of the season one league played in town while the other played across the railroad tracks. Then they would switch midseason after the all-star game. A few other backstops were scattered at the nearby schools East, West, JC Knight and Northview.

I don't remember any specifics about that first sandlot game there. That is probably a good thing. I did not get beat up though. Nobody stole my bat, glove or bike. It must have went OK based on the hundreds of games that would follow. I rarely brought a ball. Like I previously mentioned it was a special treat if someone brought a new white ball. In fact, I hardly ever remember that. I know there were several manufactures of baseballs in that day. Quality level varied a lot. But we never seemed to have to use the lower quality balls. Some would quickly deform. They would become lopsided or bust a seam. Should a ball deform like that it would be kept and cut apart for examination. To our surprise some had rubber balls at the center if you cut them open(we did). Other's had a cork. Regardless, they would quickly get grass stained and scuffed a lot at either diamond. That was another part of the pregame ritual to pick the best ball.

My vocabulary was growing leaps and bounds and not for the better. I remember my grandparents shocked look after I let out a sailor's r-rated rant against my brother. I know the older guys laughed when they heard about this. My grandpa snickered a bit- probably recalling his old navy days. My grandmother made certain I knew that was inappropriate. The older guys knew all the best dirty jokes and swore like sailors. There was some extreme creativity involved in that process. As the summer wore on I guess word had got out and the number of players kept growing. At some point we did start playing at the LL diamond at least for part of that summer. I remember some of the older guys would sometimes hit one over the fence and if you were in the outfield you had to jump the fence since nobody wanted to wait till you went out the gate and around. A few guys could leap the fence. Others like me used our arms first. Then leg up upon the bar at the top of the fence, then over. Going out the gate in left field wasn't practical. The gate didn't open and close so easily. The fence jumping was a badge of honor. That was an important skill

I quickly acquired. The younger guys typically were assigned OF roles. It seems like I was in left field a lot. If enough players showed there would be two OF's one in left center and one in right center. One guy who lived just across 7th St he was an exception he was an older guy who loved playing the outfield and despised playing infield or even pitching. He would gladly forgo playing shortstop to play LF. Whatever position you played nobody wanted to see an error. Every throw had better go to the right base and be on target. Doing something well did not necessarily bring any praise from the older guys. You wanted to get in and bat. Scores would usually reach high numbers..25-20 or so. So it was not uncommon for the batting team to bat around the order several times. On those dog days of August nobody in the field liked that much. Therefore you would hear about it if you had missed a ball, or made a bad throw. You really wanted to do things that impressed the older guys. Nobody really kept stats. The score was fairly accurately kept, that was about it. Through the course of the summer those that were getting better moved up in the draft order as well as the batting order. Base on balls or getting hit by a pitch didn't usually get you to first in sandlot play.

In the afternoons(hopefully late afternoons) some days a car would come and drag a large piece of fence(I think it was) over the infield of the real LL diamond. In the times we were there then we had to stop and allow that to happen. It didn't take long. This process turned up many stones which between pitches we would toss over the fence. Maybe it was us who gave the city the idea of putting down crushed stone. If they lined the field with the chalk lines we were done. The afternoon crowd was often times a completely different group than the morning group. But again that first year I don't remember playing too much on that field. I think sometimes we went over there when a larger number of players showed up. It also maybe the result of being chased off and warned not to. I'd guess we messed up the chalk lines that were put for the LL games. That year for sure we never played on the Pony League diamond. Bases seemed like they were a country mile apart. There was a real mound which I think was slightly closer than that of a high school pitching distance of 60 feet and 6 inches. I know those summers the Cubs were on TV(WGN I think) then. Jenkins, Holtzmann, Santo, Kessinger, Beckert, Hundley and Banks and company. Some afternoons I would get interested in one of those games and watch especially if it was raining. When I was 11 and I started pitching they didn't want me playing all afternoon anyway. We did have a babysitter at our house in those days. The only thing I remember having for lunch was hotdogs-boiled. Hotdogs, chips and maybe a few snacks were the typical lunch du jour. I think our preferred drink was koolaid. Next door neighbor and his family had sodas a lot. They always had cases on hand. I guess in event of a nuclear attack you didn't want to get caught short on that. Regardless, it was probably cooler outside with some breeze than it was in the house. There was no air conditioning in those days at least not in our neighborhood. We did have a fan or two though which ran mostly in the evenings.

I think there was also typically a game on the B&W TV either Saturday or Sunday afternoon. By the end of that year on the sandlot, I was even playing some infield and even pitching if some older guys didn't show up. Sandlot ball had no division lines. There you were playing side by side with guys from other competition in your own little league. At other times the selected teams would pit you against players off your own team. Almost daily a new guy would show up. I am not sure if other guys who played think as much of those days as I do/have. I tend to think those days were somehow ingrained in most of our minds. I have asked questions of a couple former players in putting this together. To my surprise many details are remembered fondly and accurately. It was a special time for all.

We all should certainly be in debt to our parents and for a time that allowed for us to play. We also are in great debt to the brave young men who fought communism in Vietnam. Today can you imagine parents letting their kids ride a bike alone for 7/8 blocks and being gone for 4 and even 8 hrs at a time? Today's times are even scarier and certainly more dangerous in many ways. On the sandlot it was a different world. There might have been some stress in little league. Any problems at home would soon melt away in the summer sunshine. But on the sandlot, I don't remember any stress. Even at an older age I always felt the most relaxed on the ball field. You played how you played that day. Tomorrow was another day. I have heard some hall of fame bound players talk about being able to let those bad days go. Another commentator called it "grit". I define "grit" as the process of working mistakes and failure out of your game. I know that first year many a morn I didn't necessarily want to get up eat and head over to the ball field. However, I did. Anyone who came to get me I wasn't going to say no to. That year and all subsequent years I was often the guy riding my bike gathering up a few more players. Usually riding down "C" st and collecting those guys first. I haven't explored any weather data but it seemed every day was hot and humid in those summers. There was a water fountain available next to the real LL field. We drank straight from it. Nobody I know of ever got sick. For that matter, we all also drank from the hose at home. During play when you got out of the field and weren't batting or on deck you could hustle over to the fountain and get a quick drink. Like I mentioned not all guys wore ball caps. We certainly hadn't heard of sunblock. I do remember those Coppertone signs at the convenience store where the dog is pulling those girls bathing suit bottoms down. Players just wore lose fitting clothes. Maybe once in a while a few wore cutoffs too. I don't recall shorts being worn that much. On hot days sometimes guys did remove their t-shirts. It wasn't like this group slid into base on close plays. Maybe there were a few who slid once in a while. I guess shirts stayed on for the most part since their removal opened up the sunburn situation and playing would be uncomfortable.

Hopefully at this point you are forming a picture of a typical sandlot day. I briefly mentioned a couple of the regulars from that time. Another guy I remember I think lived on the corner of 7th and East South "F". He was older. I am not sure how old but I remember hearing maybe the following year he joined the Navy. He used to wear a white T-shirt w a pack of cigarettes rolled up in the left sleeve. Much like later some rockstars could smoke and play guitar. He would smoke and play sandlot ball once in a while. He had some serious "guns". By "guns" I mean biceps. I am not sure if he is the first I saw hit a homerun over the LL fence but he likely may have been. But he was one of the first for sure. While most of us sported the haircut of the day- the pineapple as it was called. Rob had longer bushy hair. Most of the other older guys were a bit scared of him. I remember he didn't have a great arm...or at least an accurate one. I think he usually borrowed someone's ball glove. I think he was a lefty and wore the glove reversed. As I think back to the guys who regularly played that first year there was a high degree of variance in skills. Some could throw hard but not accurately. Some could catch almost any fly ball. Some hit for power but also flew out a lot. Some could not hit a curve to save their life. So speaking of the curve, at nine I had already learned how to throw one(not very well though and not the right way). Throwing a curve as they do in the majors I don't think is nearly as stressful on the elbow as throwing it the wrong way which many kids do. I rarely pitched in sandlot at that age anyhow. Many things were ahead of me. Some would be good and some bad. Looking a bit ahead, at age 10 in little league after sustaining an injury to my right knee(sliding across a bent corner of home plate) my catching days were numbered. Plus since my dad had quite a pitching reputation I think I did start pitching a little at age 10. Between practice(team and with my dad after work) my skills were increasing. This all you might say was learning the game by immersion. They say if you really want to learn a foreign language go live there a while.

I think my first glove that year was made by Franklin -I think a Bill Mazeroski model. I'd guess that would be a shorter finger infielder variety. Bill was a Pittsburg second baseman I believe. I remember putting this Camillio Pascal sticker on it. He was a pitcher famous for his curve. Mine was "broken in" mostly by just playing catch and maybe rubbing some kind of oil into the pocket. Others would pound the pocket of the glove with a mallet. I also heard of just using a ball and repeatedly tossing it into the pocket. In fact, I heard of all kinds of wild things like soaking them in salt water. That didn't seem like a good idea. It didn't take long for me though and a well defined pocket was forming. I guess in many ways so was my game. I would be taking those skills and playing some form of ball for many years to come. Nobody on the sandlot had a catcher's mitt or a first baseman's mitt. It seems like most had the long fingered outfield variety. These were fine for pitching or outfield play. As I mentioned about Rob it was not uncommon for someone not to have a ball glove and need to borrow one from the batting team. The problem came in if that person was left handed and only right handed gloves were available. As I mentioned with Rob it was there I saw mitts worn backwards on the "wrong" hand. If they were flexible enough it wasn't a huge problem. I am guessing I only owned three up through high school. A guy develops a relationship with his glove. I think I remember reading a story of a young Brooks Robinson who slept with his ball glove.

Looking back and seeing all the changes in media, programming, and technology in general it is amazing that baseball has remained relatively untouched. Some would say with the American Leauge designated hitter, or more teams, and more games that it has changed plenty. Certainly it has not changed as much as technology has. Of course some might point to player's salaries. Maybe they have changed a lot.

Chapter 2

"Same fields but evening.. 1967 first year of Little League"

In the last chapter, I discussed a little about life surrounding sandlot ball. School, current events, and sandlot ball surely set the biggest stage that being the first year of little league. I mentioned earlier I had been drafted by the Yankees. In that day we were a solid team featuring one of the league's best 3B/pitcher. I know as a freshman on the Mississinewa high school team this same player was a senior and our team's starting 3B and one of the top couple hitters. We had a couple other last year guys who were also strong players. Typically teams didn't have more than 4 twelve year olds. The Yank's coaches' son was the SS. Nowadays many leagues have what are called "major's"

and "minors". The minors are ages 9 and 10. Typically there is quite a bit of difference in terms of physical size between the age groups. In my day as was the case on the sandlots everyone all ages were welcome. I remember my first at-bat against the Cubs I believe. As was usually the case the pitcher was a 12 year old. I batted leadoff. I remember being somewhat shocked at that. I watched three straight fastballs all called strikes. I didn't even swing. Good morning, good afternoon, and goodnight. I know I was scared. Scared hitters don't do well. Horrible, I remember that clearly even today. The opposing pitcher would later be a solid SS as a Senior on that same first year high school team... He did pitch some as I recall and a couple times in practice. He certainly had a fine arm as well. Every high school practice when I saw him I would remember that strikeout. Someday I may get Alzheimer's but probably will still remember that first strike out. As I recall, my LL season started with a few games of no hits. I was also unfortunately collecting a few more strikeouts in LL. Even if I didn't get any hits, the following day on the sandlots I would collect some. Toward the end of the first half season though something clicked. Ironically, "click" is the sound of a solid base hit. I had adjusted to the faster speeds and had a two hit game against our rival team the Pirates. I think a big kid in his last year was the pitcher. That same year on a mission to round up players, I remember I came across him nearby while he was out in the yard. He was working in the yard so I didn't say anything. But I felt like he sorta gave me – the pitcher's evil eye. Pitcher's didn't like anyone hitting them let alone a 9 yr old. Confidence was building, confidence is at the core of hitting. The mental side of hitting is a deep and complex thing. Whole art of pitching seeks to capitalize on that. The first hit any season and any league is an important milestone. I think I remember each of them at every level. In LL that year I know it was a solid well hit ball up the middle. I think the next hit was a double to right center. I followed that with another 2 hit game against the Senators. All of a sudden I had a batting average. Then the second half of the season I added a few more hits. I was now back to being a regular usually playing OF maybe a little second too. One unfortunate thing I fortunately don't recall too well involved playing the outfield. A ball was hit off the fence which I ran and got. The SS(coach's son) had came out for the cutoff. I threw it hard, hard enough that it somehow hit him in the forehead and knocked him out. Not sure if he was trying to throw before he had the ball or what. Maybe he was way closer than he needed to be, I really don't recall. Likely he just took his eye off the ball. Whatever, he was unconscious and ended up with both eyes black. In the playing of the game of baseball that is one thing you are likely to get one or two of that's a black eye. Black eyes and taking a ball into the crotch area are both highly likely to occur sometime no matter how good a fielder you are. Overall, that season I could clearly measure the caliber the 12 yr olds were relative to the older guys that played on the sandlots daily. In general, they all had more well rounded skills. We couldn't catch the Senators that year. I had learned a lot from our own pennant race and believe we finished second that year. If I am correct in our AL the Senators won that year. In the National League the Cardinals won.

That year a fine team from our league, the NL champs the Cardinals made it to the final game in the big tournament in larger town nearby. I remember going and parking in the OF to watch it. I am not positive now but it might have been raining some. They played a team called Anaconda..sounded very menacing. From my own sandlot play there were 3 or 4 players my age on that team. I later would have them as teammates in Pony League and some in HS as well. I don't recall too much of that specific game except I realized that other cities had some darn good ball players too. This city was large enough to even have more than one league. As I remember they had a more realistic type of uniform. Not just T-shirts and some with ball pants. Watching this game also made it clear that our own National League had some very fine ball players. Now I wish I would have been over to at least watch the other league when they were in Gas City and our league was playing the early game across the river.

That year the Yankee team was introduced to another ritual that went with winning games. This involved driving to the Frostop root beer stand across the river. For the record, there were a couple ice cream places in Gas City. They might have been closer but neither was my top choice. Some teams only went to get a treat if they won. Others had restrictions on the size of the treat. For example, a small drink as opposed to a large. Believe me after a hot day on the sandlot everyone of us preferred a large. Everyone would pile into the back of a pickup truck(if lucky) or a few in the back seat of cars. No seat belts and no one died. Cars were bigger then. The root beer stand was a dull white irregularly shaped building with a lot of windows. It overlooked the middle school . The most striking detail I seem to remember is the sign having a large over flowing mug of foam topped root beer. The "head" or foam top is what differentiated root beer from other forms of pop(soda pop for you non-Midwesterners). We called all other soft drinks "cokes" although a few called them "sodas" unless referred to directly by their brand name. I am pretty sure I had tried a couple other root beers. But there was something really magic about the ice cold super foamy deliciousness of that cross town root beer. Since those days I have been on an unsuccessful lifelong quest to find root beer as good as that. I have tried maybe a dozen types. Some are better than others. None offer the foaminess of that. The cars could part all around the building or also along the fence. Coaches would combine to buy each member of team a root beer. At least the first year I think winning got the trip. Some others said it later was changed to going after all games but a loss meant a small rootbeer. You know I still like going to the few stands which remain. Certain occasions the coaches would spring for milkshakes at the local ice cream parlor- no complaints there either. This was located right across the street from Mississinewa high school. Root beer milkshakes and Lemon ones were variations of the normal vanilla, chocolate and strawberry all were very good. Thinking back I still preferred the root beers. I still won't turn down an opportunity to go get a nice cold frosty root beer. I wonder if kids today go somewhere to celebrate a win in their leagues.

Even as kids we would talk about major leaguers. I remember often at the root beer stand we would talk about teams and games we had seen. I could talk about major leagues with about anyone even as a nine year old. I didn't really have a favorite team then. However, my preferences were forming. I sort of liked the Tigers but also liked the White Sox. A famous pitcher for the Tigers in those days was the last 30 game winner in baseball – Denny McClain. I would later run into him at the Fort Wayne airport one time. He was everyone's favorite. And maybe he was the last 30 game winner we will see. Team choices were dominated by kids liking the only team on TV. The Cubs were on almost daily, I watched a lot of them. I likely knew more about the Cubs than any other team. I would later also see the late Ernie Banks from within a few feet at a Cub game in the early 2000s. Sadly, Ernie recently passed away. Few players will be missed as much.

Here is how the LL season broke down. In the middle of each little league season was the All-star game(s). Players from the American league played those from the National league in a couple games at each field so as to allow everyone to play. I did go over to watch part of the game at "my" nearby field that year. If I recall there was no concession stand that year. Even when the concession stand was running it certainly didn't compare to the root beer stand. But on some of those dog days in August..the small cup of "cool/lukewarm" coke was pretty darn good. Games in each league continued through the dog days of August. I am pretty sure in my last year I think the top two teams of each league played for the championship. There was no real travel ball at that age- at least for us. But we did play in a couple of tournaments in the years which followed. I don't know a lot about travel ball except that it increases the pressure on kids. It also cost the parents a lot of time and money. Sure maybe if there is some chance for a scholarship it maybe worth it.

So Little League typically ended a couple weeks before school for most players. But sandlot ball went right up through the last Friday(maybe Saturday) of the summer. Baseball was certainly most of what I did. You could call it my pastime..hoho. However, there were some non-baseball activities in the summer. As I mentioned there was bike riding on the "Grapevine" and "Dead Man's hill. I remember going to Clearwater Lake for swimming even bicycling there at least once. At Clearwater there was a covered area with a jukebox. We'd get stuff at concession stand and go there and listen to the popular music. Seems like it even played on speakers and could be heard a distance from the shelter. Some older guys played some basketball on a court they had as well. You definitely had to have shoes on because that court was sizzling hot. In the middle of the lake was the dreaded "high dive" which later I would experience(almost my last). I know I took swimming lessons at the YMCA in Marion during the winter. I learned the basics...swimming under water, floating and dog paddling. Not sure I really learned to swim at the Y though. I think it was one day at Clearwater it just registered. Plus I knew I needed to be able to swim to go into the "deeper" areas. I had even heard of people swimming across the lake. I know at that time it seemed really far.

I am pretty sure that we had a Frisbee and played with it. I know my neighbor/friend was the best Frisbee thrower. He did this unusual underhand wrist snap throw that differed from the usual across the body toss. Later we would throw forehand style and overhand too. I would later team with a great Frisbee catcher- my Border Collie Jesse!

Playing catch was a daily thing. Friends on the sandlot, after my dad got home from work, and even my mom played catch with me(at her own risk). I even played catch with myself. That year I used a stretchy nylon net in a square aluminum frame that returned your accurate throws. That is if I didn't throw it too hard(which would go through the nylon net). You didn't want to miss it either or you'd be chasing the ball a good ways. That would get old quick. Important to note the bounce off from the net didn't care if windows were in the way either. Harder throws could come back and get by me, I am sure a couple hit our aluminum siding.

Another game we played a lot was called "five dollars". A batter would choke up and punch the ball to three or four fielders standing maybe 50 ffeet away. If a fielder caught the ball in the air he banked an imaginary dollar. Catching a one hopper he banked $.75. A two hopper paid $.50. Finally any other ground ball paid $.25. However, if you made an error you lost all your money. The winner reached at least $5 and became the batter. Obviously, the game became rougher as someone got closer to $5. Another thing to note-a bad pitch meant the batter tossed the ball up and took a slightly bigger swing!

I started understanding and realizing the importance of stats in this game. Part of that learning came from accumulating/collecting baseball cards. Typical baseball card packs had 5 or 6 six cards each profiling a certain player. On the front would be his picture. On the back would be some recent statistics. I would just cringe when I got duplicates. However, even if you got duplicates the consolation prize was a good size stick of bubble gum. In those days there was also Bazooka Joe, which came with a cartoon and double bubble as well. Gum chewing was a lot bigger than today. None of us realized we were the future support of dentists everywhere. I would see a few over my life time. I started learning players and statistics of many of the major league teams. I know I did not have a huge number of cards that year. The duplicates I later found made a cool engine like sounding "click" sound when positioned just right on the bike frame so as to flip off the spokes of your bike.

So as with sandlot ball and the first year of little league was as they say in the books another year of school loomed ahead. The season had ended with the Yanks in second place. I had become a starter in either the outfield or at second base. The playgrounds of the early fall had a new topic of conversation. The guys got together for their "reindeer" games at recess to recount the summer ball playing adventures.

Chapter 3

Wild, wild ...Baseball memories- 1968

Looking back 1968 seemed a lot like 1967. There seemed to be an increasing amount of civil unrest. That was the year Martin Luther King would be shot. Also Robert F Kennedy was shot. I remember sitting on the steps of city hall his train stopped and a car drove him down Main Street. I was handed a B&W photo with his signature. I kept that for many years. Other "sit-ins" were staged at some universities. "Hey Jude" of the Beatles was the billboard top song that year. Other one's I recall that were big hits included "Harper Valley

A", "Sittin on the Dock of the Bay", "Sunshine of your Love" and "Born to Be Wild". I don't remember anything too significant through 4th grade. I do remember for some reason(I guess jealousy) I broke all the newly sharpened pencils this girl had. I got a couple whacks for that. Worst part was my neighbor was walking down the hallway and saw me and the teacher talking. It wasn't likely this would go unnoticed by the parents. They had their own network and passed information they hear on. Although I didn't follow the NFL I knew the Packers won their second Superbowl.

The following summer I would be playing as a 10 year old. I had grown some. I know on the sandlots I was hitting the ball with some authority. I remember being picked a bit higher by the captains. In LL, I also was periodically playing infield and even pitching a little. My dad had me working on my windup in front of a mirror. I was certainly a more natural infielder. Over the years there wasn't a position I didn't play. On the little league diamond I started the year as catcher. Most memories of catching weren't so good. I remember having troubles back there. Passed balls, wild pitches you name it. It is not an easy task watching the ball when the bat swings. I am pretty sure I was blinking. The mask itself can be a hindrance-especially on those foul popups. Foul tips and wild pitches both have a way of finding a spot with no padding- it was amazing the bruises. Compound bruises were typical-bruises on top of other bruises. I had purple and yellow ones through that half of the year. The chest protector and shin guard were also a real pain in the butt. Between innings usually one of assistant coaches would assist with the chest protector. Another would also go out to warm up the pitcher. I would keep the knee/shin guards on till right before I got up to bat. Then once off the bases I scrambled to find the mask, chest protector and shin guards and get them on for the next inning in the field. Eventually, I could do that in a reasonable amount of time. Seemed I was always on base that year. It was my highest batting average year in little league.

You wear a lot of sweat and dirt as a catcher. It at least covers some of your multicolored bruises. I probably could have eventually been a good or at least decent catcher. I was flexible, had a good arm, and could hit. But I am certain I did not like it. Always had a lot of respect for all catchers from that point on. At the higher levels you had to call a good game too. I guess that takes some intelligence which relative to some I guess I had. With all the chess I played in later years some would say I was tactical and very much a strategist- both essential skills required by a good catcher. It is for that reason some catchers go on to be fine major league managers. Catchers usually come to the mound and offer their judgment for the use by the manager when a pitcher is having trouble. In little league mound visits were usually to tell the pitcher to calm down and take his time. I believe calling a good game would have come with time too. However, my catching came to an end after injuring my right knee sliding across a bent home plate corner. The doctor thought since I was young it would heal. I think I iced it a lot the first couple days. After the injury, I tried catching a style called "Sanguillen style". That means the right leg is extended instead of being in a full squat. I had limited success with that. However, that limits your ability to throw. Much better catchers were waiting behind me for a chance. Regardless the knee just burnt like fire trying to squat in that fashion. The doctor had said it would probably heal in time. It probably did for the most part heal. Today they probably would have done an MRI or CT scan and arthoscopically repaired it. Well as an old codger now, I can say it healed to a point but remained much like after the injury. Maybe not as quite as bad as at that time though. I am sure there was ligament/tendon damage.

Behind the plate may have been a tough row to hoe that year. But as a hitter at the plate I was killing the ball. I remember hitting two doubles off the fence one game against the Cubs. The next game was against the Tigers and one of the league's best pitchers. Again I hit two doubles off the fence. The following Thursday while waiting on our game I was at the backstop watching. All of a sudden there was someone standing by me. It was that Tiger pitcher. He came up and with that "evil eye" glaring said.. "heh those balls you hit off me- that was just luck right?" I didn't really know how to answer. I think I agreed for sake of an argument or worse. The first half of the season came to a close. I remember the coaches handing out ballots or at least voting. I think since we weren't too good we had to vote for only two. I was the leading hitter so I was sure one would be me. I remember the crushing feeling when two other names were announced. After which the coach told me I deserved it. I got over it(I think). I wasn't aware of it at the time but my vision was changing I guess as I was growing. I was becoming near sighted. Even so I was hitting the ball like crazy. Glasses and I mean goofy ones.. were just what I didn't need. The wire rims were sorta popular but prone to bending of the frames. I know I was pitching some that year after I had hurt the knee. It didn't hurt to push off and throw toward home. The knee was really only an issue for squatting.

That season was interrupted when an opportunity to ride out to California with my grandparents came up. That meant missing like 3/4 games. It was a long hot drive. My middle brother Matt came as well. I believe we left late one night. We slept in the back and I believe my grandfather drove across the center of the country at least 16 straight hrs that first day. This was a good plan for him because I know we were loud and fought across the country. I am not sure if that was the first year we played "slug bug" or not. If so I am sure that was irritating. In fact they may have got a nomination for sainthood. Every motel was an adventure. They usually had pools or so we lobbied for. I remember near Vegas my grandfather took me into some restaurant or bar. I think I saw my first one arm bandit even pulled the arm. I guess a kid going into a bar was OK in those days. A couple things stick out about that trip. I distinctly remember a crop dusting plane diving at us. I think my grandpa fell asleep a couple times on the way there but somehow woke up in time that there was no accident. I remember being stuck in traffic in California for a really long time near a bridge. I am sure it was over 4 hrs completely stuck no moving. But we finally reached our destination which I believe was Merced. We were visiting his brother Everett. We stayed with some family that had a boy near my age. I remember playing some catch. But I think he called it pitch. That is messed up. I know we were there a couple days. We came back to Indiana the southern route. We visited the Grand Canyon and Hoover Dam. Don't think we even had a camera. It's possible my parents have a few old pictures but I don't recall. I also think we stopped in Missouri at some cave famous for being a Jesse James hideout. I wouldn't be surprised especially out west if we weren't driving 80+. That season our team had not done so well. I think I missed 3 or 4 games. But one might have been rained out. I always thought if I could time travel it would be cool to return and play those games. I doubt it would have mattered much since we weren't contending. We might have finished 4th or 5th. I think I had my highest LL batting average that year. I was just over .666. I was not in love with the glamour of a homerun yet. I always was a line drive hitter.

That summer I remember I had been saving all the money I had for some time. Not sure why or what for. The guy who took over a large part of the catching duties helped me figure out the what-for part. The carnival had come to town and landed in local grocery parking lot. They were a couple blocks to the east of our house. There were rides and other fun stuff. They even had a Ferris wheel, a tilt-a-whirl and who knows what else. But we were hooked on these machines/games called cranes(claw game). Right up front near the window were the best prizes. You know the pocket knives and $50 bills. I think I blew pretty much all I had saved. I think I had around $18 which in those days was almost a fortune. I think the cranes were a quarter. Shoot they might have been a dime. Since I was "loaning" money to my buddy too we didn't get a great number of tries. I do remember the carnival operator handing us each 4 quarters(dimes)- probably out of guilt. I'm not sure but they might have taken tokens instead of cash. I know the later versions did. Dozens of try's resulted in nothing good. We each had our technique on playing the cranes.

You see it took timing. You couldn't exactly read the crane position before dropping the "jaws" it took some timing. Also it could only be positioned moving only once to the side and once toward the front of the machine. Then you dropped the crane toward the "goodie" you wanted. We had won a few trinkets each though and a lot of fun. We even had some close calls with the good stuff too. I remember walking home and my buddy saying "you think your parents might give you a couple bucks". Pretty sure they did and back we went. It was hardly worth the walk over there though. My buddy was a small but tough solid player. I also think it was that year that he threw a ball when I wasn't looking and hit me squarely in the eye. So along with all the other bumps and bruises I had a "shiner". For the record, I think he also hit my dad in the eye with one. A "shiner" wasn't so bad a couple days after. Everyone thought you got it in a fight or something. I remember my barber commenting on it. I learned it was anticlimactic to say you were hit by a ball when you weren't looking. A fight was a lot more interesting. My buddy's older brother was also our shortstop that year. My dad had taken over after the original manager had given up the reins of coaching as his son had moved up to Pony league. The Yankees were improving.

That summer, I remember being over at a another friend's house(of the Pirate assistant coach I believe) when the rival Pirate's coach came to drop off some equipment. I didn't know him..but he knew me. He said.. "heh don't you play for the Yankees. I said "I did". He said, "how many hits did you get against us?" Thought for a minute and said "4/5". He said well I am glad we don't have to pitch to you anymore. I said "why is that". He said," well because you are moving up to Pony League". That confused me a bit. I then said, "no I am only 10- I have two more years". I guess now he was teasing me... but maybe not. The Pirates were a rival then and would be the next two years. The Pirates were a good team which I knew several of the players from playing on the sandlots. My neighbor/best friend was a Pirate. Another friend down the street was also a Pirate. The three of us even played high school ball together. The following year, the next time we played our team beat them 14-2. I pitched and homered and doubled in that game as an eleven year old. I guess their coach even liked that less.

I had discovered baseball cards and comic books that year. The baseball cards were available at the local pantry/food mart as well as the at the grocery. Comic books were at the local newsstand. There were no camera's in those days and the baseball cards especially were all too available. It was too easy to slip a couple packs in your pocket or shirt. I found if I bought a couple packs it prevented any suspicion. Comic books from the old newsstand were also up for grabs too. Another skill I seemed to have. I think that was the first year I had nearly a complete set of baseball cards. Each pack of baseball cards came with a stick of bubble gum. I remember stacks a few inches high setting on my dresser. Maybe it was a lesson in Karma but the gum chewing would pay me back many times over. I chewed the gum constantly which resulted in several fillings. One of which was deep and in a molar on the lower right side. I am pretty sure that exact tooth has troubled me the rest of my life. Also has cost me a lot more than the baseball cards I lifted from the stores around town. That first filling was my worst all time dental experience. It was incredibly painful.

Thinking back I know I had a couple shots to start it off. They didn't put the stuff on the gums in that day. Plus I am certain the dentist missed the nerve completely. It also seemed to take forever. I know I got angrier with each passing minute. Round two of Novocain shots didn't help either. Eventually the ordeal ended. Or had it just begun? My face was the size of a pumpkin- or so it felt. After it was finally over I remember standing up and punching him straight in the stomach doubling him over. It was the best upper cut I ever threw. The paybacks were hell Karma again? I guess payback was what I was thinking toward him anyway. I calmly went out into the lobby looking over my shoulder a couple times. It wasn't over quite yet -my dad was at the desk paying. I think it was the only time he brought me to the dentist. For some reason the desk part took forever longer than normal. I swear I saw the clock tick backwards not once but twice! I glanced at the elevator ..it looked so far and seemed to be getting farther by the second. I glanced down the hallway expecting to see the dentist. I wanted to just make a break for it. Just go and head out to the car. If I could just make the elevator I might just get out of this. I did feel a bit bad. Well escape was not to happen. Plus I think I had to go apologize. Plus tell the dentist it wouldn't happen again. Well I may have said that but didn't believe it so I guess that was a lie. Another mess up like that by him and I could make no guarantees. I had some experience with the apology thing before. So I had that routine down. Once I had taken some gum at the dime store. My parents then made me go pay and apologize. Still, to this date I believe he deserved what he got. I bet even today he tells this story. The next thing I recall I think one of the assistants came up and told my dad about it. I knew I was in trouble nonetheless but we had made the elevator. I think there was a deafening period of silence. I know I had to explain. I was shall we say "warned". Keep in mind I could punch pretty well too -used the whole body. From that point on the dentist was ready and had his assistants hold my arm(s) during future procedures and until he was safely out of the room. The old Pastor's story "Lead me not into temptation, cause I don't have a problem finding it all on my own" definitely seemed to apply.

In those days I was a big reader of comic books. They were also at the local barber shops. In fact, it was there I got to read some that were not my usual favorites. I liked the Avengers, Fantastic Four, Captain America, Iron Man, Hulk, but mostly I liked Spiderman. You can imagine now I when see these characters on the movie screen what a critic I am. I know every slight difference from the original comics. Peter Parker was a guy who liked chemistry and physics. To me the villains were a lot better in the comics and never done well in the movies which followed years later. My favorite villain though had to be the Green Goblin. Behind Spiderman the Fantastic Four was a probably close second. They introduced the Silver Surfer who I really liked. But FF4 villain Dr Doom was maybe even a better villain than the Goblin. I did not read the DC comics much. But sometimes that was all there was at the barber shop. A few of those I remember were Justice League, Aquaman, Batman, Superman, Wonder Woman, Sgt Fury even Archie. Strangely, I did like reading Archie. There was even a cartoon about Archie which later featured their top hit "Sugar, Sugar". Back to superheros- I mean come on who wouldn't like super powers. I remember ending up with a laundry basket full of comic books. The laundry basket was kept behind the furnace in out utility room. Years later after hearing they had some value I went to get them. Unfortunately, they had been thrown out. Probably it was karma again adjusting things.

I was also a regular at attending vacation bible school and Sunday school in the years prior and during my LL days. I guess that helped keep me from getting too bad. Our church was just down the street. Both Sunday school and vacation bible school had cookies, crackers and kool aid. I remember the teachers would bring out a tray with small cups of kool aid and snacks and napkins. I also liked the bible teaching. I still remember my wonderful teachers from those early years. One early memory I had from years prior involved the teacher rescuing me. One gal a teacher's helper(a local girl from a block away) came to my rescue. We were all setting in these fold-up pews for our lesson. I am not sure exactly how I managed to get my finger(s) stuck in the open area at the bottom back of the fold down pew seat. I was unable to get off the pew to fold it back up. The other kids had left the room. I was stuck. They had even shut off the light. The teachers aid glanced in and came and lifted it for me. I don't think I ever thanked her. Not sure why I didn't yell for help. I didn't call for help but struggled to no avail. She passed away at much too young an age of cancer recently. She was a wonderful Christian lady. There were quiz games and other stuff I liked.

In spite of all my troubles, being 10 wasn't so bad. It seemed like a time of great discovery and adventure. In addition to baseball, It was a time of bb guns, model rockets and adventure. I guess every incident had some kind of lesson to learn. Baseball cards had statistics on the back I became quite knowledgeable on the players in the majors. I learned division and fractions were involved in figuring batting average. Therefore math was important. I memorized fractions and knew about ratios. In 4th, 5th and 6th grades one thing I liked in school was called SRA reading. It involved these large color coded folders that had what seemed like an endless amount of great stories. You would read one and I think answer some questions. You would move up to higher levels as you got through particular levels. They were color coded. It seems like I was reading stuff on 8th grade or freshman level. I loved reading. Speaking of reading, in the year prior back in 3rd grade I still remember our teacher reading "Charlotte's Web". You could hear a coin drop as she read. I remember walking home each day talking about what happened with my brother and friend. Then the day that Charlotte died. Not sure I ever really got over that completely. I really think my interest in reading started that year. I would also order books. I had discovered science fiction. I would order these books which would come a couple weeks later. Books were usually about dinosaurs, space, robots, and time travel.

The sandlots still continued almost daily. I am sure the variation of players was also growing. We were playing regularly at the LL diamond. I know it was that year I did hit one over the fence in one of those games. I still mostly played in the outfield in sandlot play. I would later play some OF as a freshman in HS. I always could catch a fly ball. I did love throwing on runners too. That was evident one season of slow pitch in Maryville, TN where I threw out dozens. Threw for the cycle once getting at least one at every base. I doubt many have done that.

I remember returning to school that fall. Many of the boys in my class also played Little League. Several were in the National League. It was sort of a brag fest for everyone. I think their teams had done well that year again. Our team did not win much but was improving though. If I am correct it was the Tigers that were the best team that year. The Senators and Pirates of our league as I mentioned were also the standards of our league then. Both would be tough in the two years coming up too. By this time I was doing fine in school. Maybe baseball taught me more than a few lessons. In fact, many lessons of life can be learned from baseball -a few of which I have mentioned. Among them I am sure I learned about preparation, structure, rules, organization, and strategy. In fact, 5th grade would be very enjoyable. I remember late in the year our teacher had us out to her farm. I don't recall a lot more from that year. But a new summer of great adventures was just ahead. I think we still had recess then. Seems like we played games like tag and maybe some kickball and/or dodgeball. I know I crossed the hand over hand monkey bar type thing on the playground. I couldn't do that before. Honestly, I don't remember getting in trouble at all in 5th grade. But that seems pretty unlikely. At least I didn't do anything too notable. I guess I was learning some about life. I am pretty sure that was the year my grandfather died. I had so many memories of being at his house. I remember climbing their tree. I remember getting sick eating too many apricots. He was a carpenter. When I was little maybe even two I would name all the tools. I am sure he always thought I would become a carpenter.

Chapter 4

Summer of 69... memories- Season 3

This was the year of Woodstock. I knew nothing of Woodstock at the time other than maybe seeing a picture in the paper, on a magazine cover, or maybe on the news. But I had been buying 45s. For those who don't know these were 6" vinyl records. A couple summers down the road and I would join the famous(infamous) Columbia House record club. It was great as you got to pick out like thirteen free records but then had to buy one a month for the next year(or few months). My first was Woodstock. Woodstock counted as 3 as I remember. Once you finished your commitment you could get another free record for resigning up. Most people did. The local stores didn't carry a large selection. I however think I passed on that option. I had discovered a small audio store in Marion called "Big D's". I could afford a couple 45s each week either from Big D's or nearby grocery. That years top hits included "Sugar, Sugar" by the Archies! Also "Aquarius Let the Sun Shine In", "Honky Tonk Women" and "Crimson and Clover". A popular style of art and also music of the time was known as psychedelic . Wikipedia defines it as to make visible or reveal. Drugs like LSD may have been inspiration to this culture as well. It still seems funny with all the great classic rock bands that "Sugar, Sugar" a song based on a cartoon/sung by comic characters was the year's top song. A downside to buying albums was that some had only one or two songs you liked and a lot you didn't.

1969 was also the golden year(sorta) for the Chicago Cubs. The Mets went on to win the World Series after catching and surpassing the Cubs. The Cubs had led until late in August and September. The Cubs had several Hall of Fame players. It seemed unbelievable at the time. Maybe more incredible is the Mets went on to beat Atlanta and then defeat the powerful 1969 Oriole team in the World Series. Other than maybe the '90 Reds that was one of the more shocking WS wins of my lifetime.

Of course this was the summer that the moon landing was televised in July. Tang had been made and drank by John Glenn. I remember seeing stacks of tang at the grocery. A new form of food called space sticks had hit the stores. These were derived from a actual smaller sized food brought into space. We all liked them but none more than my brother Brian. I remember having cases of those. Although several flavors were available I think we mostly bought chocolate. I think we bought a space blanket that year as well. Not sure if NASA got any kickback for these things or not. More incredibly the show Star Trek was to have its last season that year. Watergate was around the corner. Kent state shooting was only a few months off. It was definitely a time of great change.

5th grade rolled along fairly uneventful. At least until my grandfather died. I guess everyone has that first encounter with death sometime. I guess many times it seems death comes much too soon. That was the case then. I didn't realize it at the time but even that cloud had a silver lining. In fact, something wonderful happened later that spring. Following my grandfather's death I know my grandmother had been attending a small one room church in town. The small white building is still there. She was a dedicated worker in the church from that point on. I know she cleaned, cooked, and drove people to church after she learned to drive. She drove this noisy cream/rust colored subcompact. She also came to clean at our house since my mom was working. We were invited to a revival around Easter time at that same church. I had no idea what that was. I do know I didn't want to go. I exhausted every trick I had to get out of it. I think the weather was nice and believe it was Good Friday. If I am correct that would have been April 4th. It was not too unusual for a few of us to make it over to play a few games before school had let out especially on holidays and yeah Good Friday was a holiday then. I guess that shows just how popular sandlot play was. That year might have been the biggest. So there I was at the ball diamond when I see our light blue bug pulling up the road. I think that was before my dad had painted the wheels orange. With the remainder of the paint he painted the foul poles. Concerning the car, I actually drove the "Bug" a couple times a few years later when I had driver's ed. Seeing my mom coming wasn't good. I don't ever remember my parents coming to get me at the ball diamond. After a brief argument my mom won out. I know she said I had to take a bath and put on some nice clothes. Earlier in the day in fact the Pastor had come to our house and even beaten my dad in table tennis. Table tennis would be a game that stuck with me through the years. I played in college, Industrial club, then in the city club in Fort Wayne-even getting second place in the state in under 3600 doubles. But I was just a beginner in that day. He was a nice southern gentleman I believe from Oklahoma. He could play a mean game of ping pong though. I guess that had some degree of respect in my book. I put on my best grump face and off we went. It was unprecedented and unusual going to any service with my parents. It was also the first time with my grandmother. I remember getting there and seeing a couple neighbor girls of my dad's friend in the choir. They were a couple years older. That meant more interesting to me. I had been over to visit them a couple times. But singing there that day they reminded me of angels. So far so good this didn't seem too bad. I had not even been to an actual church service at this time. The small church was uncomfortably warm even in the spring. That was appropriate for the fire and brimstone message we were about to receive. It was right out of the handbook of Billy Sunday(former baseball player turned Pastor). Thinking back I can't think of another type of message that would have gotten through to me. It was clear to me that I was on the wrong side of the fence. I didn't know much about heaven but was clear I wouldn't like hell. Forever sounded like a long time..even longer than a second grade school day or longer than that service was taking. Following the sermon was the standard alter call. Almost everyone had gone up front to pray, including my dad, mom, brother, and grandmother. There I sat almost like I had my finger caught in the pew. A lady from the church who I had seen talking and praying with other people glanced at me. I of course quickly looked down. That didn't work. Nevertheless, she came up to me and asked me if I understood what the pastor was talking about. Understood? Shoot the picture was crystal clear. I had done plenty of bad things up to that point and realized exactly where I stood. The list was long. I think many people when faced with the Gospel message would agree it is true but think they will have another time. I think that is the premise of CS Lewis book the "Screwtape Letters". In that book one demon suggests that procrastination is the best way to get the most people into hell. I mean just have them believe the message but tell them they have time and just to wait. Head knowledge and heart knowledge are different. This was a time of action. I remember her telling me now is the best time. I sorta realized there may not be another chance. Things happen in life, accidents, tragedies of various kinds. She said I did not need to go down front. It was crowded down there. My father and brother were there. She asked if she could help me pray and ask Jesus into my heart and He would forgive my sins. I said yeah. I followed her as she led me in the sinner's prayer. So the kid who had stolen dozens of comic books, hundreds of baseball cards, cussed like a sailor, punched the dentist and many other things had become a sinner saved by grace! Whereas, I had controlled my bad language at home the sandlots were a different story. But that too was quickly changing. I think even a couple guys had noticed I was cleaning up my bad language. They hadn't said anything but a couple of them drifted away in terms of friendship. I also regularly started going to Sunday school down the street. Today when I see pictures of the guardian angel shaking/hanging her head reflecting

Chris M.

on her job with guiding and protecting me I reflect back on my life and think those images apply. I'm sure over the years the Holy Spirit may have thought that about me too. I even stayed a couple times for the main church service. I attended church down the street at New Hope. Years later I think around 18 or 19 I would be baptized there in that church. There was a baptistery behind the pulpit of our church. The old one room building had expanded into 3 sections by this time. Glad I hadn't waited any longer or I might have been a challenge to lift up out of the water. Over the next few years several of the sandlot and little league group would also later start attending with me. One thing about that church we had no shortage of local girls who played the piano. In fact, one friend/sandlot/LL player who graduated midterm our Sr year was the first to marry- married one of those fine pianists. Those were the days of the old gospel hymns which I still enjoy hearing today. "Nothing But the Blood", "Amazing Grace", "Blessed Assurance", and "Come Thou Fount" were a few of my favorites. I know once my SS class had a sleepover. I think boys were in one class and girls in another. I remember sleeping in the attic of the teacher's home. That morning I remember eating pancakes very early and then heading over to the famous Easter Pageant. The Easter Pageant included hundreds of choir members and actors who relived the last few days of Jesus life, death and resurrection. It was the first time I heard the "Hallelujah Chorus".

Following 5th grade sandlot play was in full swing again. In fact, I think if this year was not the peak it was close to it. We were getting 14 or 16 players on some occasions. I remember a couple times the younger ones were sent to the corner field to play. So we used than one ball field. More people meant more bats to choose from. This was the year of the home run. We played at the little league diamond almost exclusively. Some of the regular guys kept track of their homers- those that went over the fence. But after a while I wasn't serious about counting them. I think the guy who would come and get me to play most times, John was the leader though. He professed of numbers well into the hundreds. That meant a lot of fence jumping to retrieve the ball. That I can vouch for and whatever the number was I know I jumped that fence plenty of times. I hit my share but don't think I reached triple figures. I wasn't usually a captain but was once in a while that year. I remember how cracked bats were not discarded but nailed, taped, and reused. Bats in that day cracked and didn't usually break into two pieces. This was especially true if it was a really good or favorite bat. You know they still worked pretty well. We primarily used Adirondack or Louisville sluggers. They were made of white ash. Today especially in the majors the pros use hickory or maple instead. This may well be why you see so many or at least more bats break into pieces. Of course it may also have something to do with pitchers throwing 95 or more mph. In recent years I believe the ash tree supply was cut short due to the explosion of the ash borer beetles.

Bats were also somewhat customized. Some guys taped the grips of the bats. There was no pine tar or rosin on the sandlots. I also remember special dimpled glue-on-grips on certain bat handles. I know you bought them like that. Many also used sticky tape to enhance the grip. I liked it ok but was not available on the bats I liked best. While most bats were a blondish color I remember some that type of grip were two toned with the trademark to the wide end stained dark brown. Some had what they called flame tempering too. Basically flame tempering was a process that highlights the grain in the wood as well as the trademark. Thinking back I don't remember any black bats. There certainly weren't any metal bats. Technology was also finding its way into the on deck circle and to the bat itself. I am pretty sure this is the year I discovered the donut to put on the bat and swing in the on deck circle. Till that point most guys loosened up by swinging two or even three bats. Instead of multiple bats you slid a weighted donut unto the handle end of the bat. The donut was a much neater solution to swinging more than one bat. I did both though. When time to hit you would stamp the handle end and the donut came off for the next on deck hitter. After swinging the weighted bat and removing the donut the bat felt much lighter. No pipes, ceramic tubes, or winged versions then. In fact, I was the only one with a donut that I recall. I didn't bring it to the sandlot either for obvious reasons. I would guess this sandlot summer often included my middle brother Matt playing. Also other younger brothers were joining and playing as well.

In our front yard we had a small maple planted dead center of our whiffle ball field. In fact the next door neighbors did as well. These served to catch or at least slow down most of the well hit whiffle balls. So they served as fielders of sort. There were a couple types of whiffle balls used. One type had slots around one half of the ball. We didn't like those so well since their flight was limited by the airflow into the slots. The other more preferred type was a solid ball with formed seams which could be made to curve in ways which seemed to defy all aerodynamic principles… even to rise. They seemed to also be magnetic. They seemed to be attracted to the rain gutters on any house. Our roof certainly saw a few as did the neighbor's. If that roof could only talk of all the stuff that ended up on it that might be a book in itself. In a typical whiffle ball game usually only 4/5 or so played. It was pitchers hand and throw at the runner. That meant doing so around one of the two maple trees. First base was a metal lid which opened to the water meter. Second base was the second smaller maple tree in the neighbor's yard. Third was the SE corner of our house-more specifically the gutter pipe. Somehow nobody pulled it lose. Just in front of our maple was where the pitcher threw from. A catch falling from the limbs of the tree was considered an out. The ball might zig zag down the branches like the ball in a Japanese pachinko machine. A quick dive and catch meant a memorable out. Of course wind played havoc with this game. I never liked wind much in any sport. I remember one day one of my friends hit one over the two maples and over neighbor's driveway in dead center. A tape measure shot! I don't remember it being wind aided either. It was not easy even then to get it by the neighbor's tree. Some homers pulled over the left field area(neighbors house) were homers but later deemed automatic doubles. We didn't use those yellow thin plastic bats. We preferred the brown plastic roughly regulation size ones. Some of those would often become slightly curved. The knuckle was the pitch of choice for throwing wicked breaking pitches. You mix that with a rising fastball and even the best hitters would struggle. It took a certain wind to assist throwing the "riser". With a certain side and back wind "risers" could be thrown. Sometimes we put the nylon net behind the batter as a back stop. I do remember pulling one into my parent's bedroom window on more than one occasion. However, it held up as far as I remember mostly thanks to the screen. Thru the years that maple grew huge. There were four large branches coming from the main trunk. I always thought it would be cool to have a bat made from one of those. Kind of like a magic bat as in Robert Redford's movie the "Natural". The maple trees(ours and the neighbors) I have referred to were cut down a couple years ago. However the neighbor across the street still has a couple of these now giant trees. I am pretty sure I am the only one who cared they were cut down. As both were very large and produced a mountain of leaves. In these latter years the problem was there were no kids to play in the leaves anyway.

Back to the sandlot, sometimes we would find golf balls in the field. Those would always be a special treat to hit. For the most part we couldn't hit them that great. In fact, I think they tended to dent the bats. However, you want to get great practice in the outfield- try catching one of those. If you can catch them you will have no trouble with a baseball. On the toy market "superballs" had turned up. They weren't cheap. However, one day we brought one over to the diamond. It was a democratic process to choose who would hit it. Of course the oldest biggest guy was chosen. He was a good choice. He was chosen to hit it. I threw him a perfect ball which he launched dead center to the 7th street road. At least 325 feet! Of course the ball was lost in the bean field. It was probably caught in that spider's web or at least the web of one of its descendents. Later when I think I was in high school I decided it was time for me to try that. I stepped into the batter's box with a superball in hand. As I often did I probably provided some play by play such as this.. "Its all come down to this, bases are loaded and two out. Chris M presents the White Sox last hope of winning a World Series. Here is the pitch". Crack... I launched one which I lost as it sailed over the center field fence. I can't say it went as far as the first one I mentioned but I can't say it didn't. I think it was overcast and I just lost sight of it.

In other baseball related fun, I had discovered Strat-o-matic board game baseball. If you wanted one of these you had to order it from the company. Then wait to get it. Getting stuff in the mail was fun. One of my cousins had it too- he was a Red Sox fan. Another friend also had it – he was a Dodger fan. This game is played by rolling 3 dice and then referring to tables on player cards(1,2,3) or if 4, 5, 6 come up you refer to pitcher's card. So you essentially setup lineups and manage teams and play games. The first year I think I only had about eight teams. I had to go to the library to print score sheets. I don't think they charged then if they did it couldn't have been much. But I printed a lot of them. I remember a stack about 4" high. I would need most of those the following year. That following summer I actually had both leagues and played a 30 game season. I know there were fewer teams then but still that was a lot of games! But once you got the knack you could play and score a game pretty quickly. Many nights I played 20 games or more! A few times my brothers played a game or so. But mostly I played alone. I believe my champion Oriole team defeated my cousins' champion Red Sox(hmmm). Then I played my other buddy's champion Dodgers(hmm they weren't so good that year) for the ultimate title which I think I won. It was great fun though. More of a luck based game with a touch of strategy involved.

In Little League we were in a three way race for the top of the AL. I was the top pitcher which meant I always pitched against the best team we played that week. In Little League as a pitcher you are limited to 6 innings per week. One game against the Tigers I threw a no-hitter struck out 19. That might sound like an error but it is not. In a six inning little league game there would normally be 18 outs. However, if a runner reached on a third strike missed by the catcher he was still counted as a strike out. Interesting thing about that game was that we lost. Usually pitchers who throw no-hitters win. I threw hard but didn't have the best control. I think the following game I hit an opponent in the foot. Later I saw him in a cast. I felt bad. Some wildness is not necessary a bad thing. It can be used to your advantage. When I returned to playing baseball in 92 in the Men's Sr League I was in a tournament in Dayton. I threw a ball that ran in and hit the first batter in the chest. Then I really felt bad. The following hitters were pretty scared to bat. Scared hitters don't do well. I never had great control in terms of a pitcher. You will see some stats later that are a clear indication of that. Even at that time I seemed to not always agree with the umpires calls. Doubt they heard what had happened to my dentist. Maybe I should have told them.. lol. In that particular 19 strike out game we had a couple errors and at least one runner reached on a swinging third strike. Whatever the Tigers scored 2 runs. I remembered coming across that old score book in the 90s. I had two hits and scored our only run. Another interesting fact about that game came out many years later as well. Our catcher came up to me at our 20[th](I think) high school reunion. He said he wanted to tell me something. He told me he had hurt his hand that game and was "pinching" at the ball since catching it normal hurt. He said he was afraid to tell my dad about it. All these years nobody knew. He said that caused him to miss sometimes as he tried to pinch and catch balls in the webbing not the pocket. I am sure I had as much or more cause for losing that game. I remember getting off to a solid start that year. I know I recall hitting near .600. That average was several pts less than the previous year. At the season's halfway mark I was chosen for the all-stars that year.

That first all-star game didn't go well. That game was practically in my back yard. For reasons unknown to me they played me at SS. Per my recollection I made three straight errors in one inning. One ball was chopped up the middle it went into and out of my glove. It actually bent the webbing of my glove. None were easy chances as I recall. Maybe it was nerves I don't know. One was a throwing error. That came on a ball I fielded to the backhand side. Batting offered a chance of redeeming myself. But that too was not going to end well. I faced the first leftie I had ever seen. He threw a ball that tailed away from a right hander. I struck out. Once I understood his fastballs naturally tailed away I got it. I rocked most lefties from that point on. That is unless they were "soft tossers". The following game went OK at least from an error and strike out perspective. I had a sharp single in that game. The second half of the season as I previously mentioned was a down to the wire pennant race. I got my first trophy for making that all-star team but certainly didn't deserve one. From that point on every game counted. I believe the Senators came out on top. We tied the Pirates for second. My dad reminded me that he offered to play the Pirates in a tie breaker. But that didn't happen. I don't remember us playing in any tournaments following the season.

Our team featured a 9yr old Jimmie from down the street who had also played the last two sandlot seasons. Unlike most 9 year olds he was an instant starter. Playing sandlot as a 7 and 8 year old put him way ahead of most his age. He could play about every position. He threw a natural curve and I think even did some spot relief as a nine year old. Essentially every ball he threw naturally curved. Many hitters just bailed and or watched a strike go by. I am thinking that at least for part of the year he led off. I know he played some 2nd and maybe SS as well. That year my brother Matt was another 9 yr old and was seeing some playing time in the OF. Another friend lived down the street and anchored our outfield. One of our best was from the north side of town and played 3rd. He was the younger brother of our star that first year. Another "C" St guy had taken over catching at least until the hand injury. I still recall that flimsy old catcher's glove. It was the likely culprit. Earlier in the year we had lost our chief "crane player/ catcher" as his family had moved. This was also the year of brothers as we had 3 younger brothers all from "C" St join the team. Another of the regular sandlot gang from "D" st also played. Several of this group that I have mentioned lived right on "C" St. I think the following year our sandlot group became known as the south side "C" street gang. One person coined us the "Cruds". One big event either that year or the following one was when the "Cruds" travelled by bike to the north side to play a group of guys from that side of town. That was perhaps our version of travel ball. As I recall we had a lot of fun but lost a close one. I remember talking about how we could have won if we had this guy or that guy ect. The sandlot phenomenon was going on there too!

Just going door to door on "C" street could round up several players. Along with the regulars which included myself it was certain you could round up 8-10 just from "C" st. Sometimes guys would fan out one heading down to "F" street another to "B" ect. Usually we did not go north of Main street. Although each day the players changed I'd say this gang had now become the core group. Sometimes players from north of Main would show up. Other's a couple or several blocks away were also routinely becoming regular's too.

A couple significant things happened at the nearby ball park. A concession stand was built behind the backstop. I think that was the year that my dad painted the foul poles orange. As I mentioned that orange might have been leftover from painting the bug's wheels. In the field behind was an old trailer which sometimes provided shelter if a shower came through. It was either there or the cement dugouts

Chris M.

of the pony league field. They had built a small concession stand that year I think it was. The concession stand was always locked. For the most part the pony league field next door loomed empty calling to us. The field seemed like it was gigantic. We never played there that year. The home run counts all would have dramatically went down that is for certain. I also think crushed stone was put in between the little league and Pony league ball diamonds. I guess the times were indeed a changing.

I have mentioned various other activities. Well some I am not so proud of. We would often ride our bikes and cross Main Street to go to the Pantry. I mentioned baseball cards being a particular target. That was still true. I knew it wasn't right but it was a habit. Same is true with cigarettes also. I tried smoking a couple times but usually just coughed a lot. They were good to offer to the older kids. A couple times we even stole beer- right from the truck. That too we didn't like too well. I think that is the year that a pinball machine showed up at the Pantry. After a while I got respectable at pinball on that machine. Had learned to use flippers individually and also to get targets for more pts and longer play ect. I think that year I was also in a bowling league at the ally's on Main Street. For the most part I wasn't a real good bowler. But my parents got me a ball. I think I was maybe around a 109 or so average. However, one day the stars aligned. I bowled a 215 and a 165 and a 115. By far that stood out for me. With the usual handicap pts our team won easy. I remember the following week waiting on the door to open my captain asked me if I had another 500 series in me. Don't know what I answered but I didn't. In all these years(I don't bowl) I am positive that I never bowled another 200+ game. One classmate Dale was and still is an exceptional bowler. For the most part this was a vastly different crowd than those at the little league fields. But it was a cool place on hot days. I think we bowled only once a week.

One of the pair of brothers on the team just down the street had a pool. Not every afternoon was baseball at the sandlot. I remember some afternoons after playing all morning I would get invited over to swim. Usually had to run home and get some trunks. It seemed we would then ride our bikes up to his father's gas station and get a soda or something to drink and then back to his house. It was pool cleaning time. After that we could swim and dive a while. Usually by 3:00 or so I had to head home. Our dinner time was 330 sharp. That is when my dad got home from work. It seems like "Gilligan's Island" was on about that time. During these years I did have a baby sitter. She would be home with our younger brother. Usually she would have lunch when we showed up. My neighbor's mother was famous for being able to call him from a block away at his lunch time. Another special treat was the ice cream truck. Nothing carried quite the urgency of hearing the musical tune and yelling "The ice cream truck, the ice cream truck". One time I remember the baby sitter giving me money to get two ice creams one for me and one for my brother. Running down to the truck I dropped part of the money. I could only buy one..which I ate on the way back home. I got back and was in trouble. Next time I had to go down and get one just for him. Another lesson in what selfishness gets you I guess.

The final things that had highlighted the summer were bonfires in the evenings at the neighbors across the street. Many times these were accompanied by sleep outs. Not sure a lot of sleeping took place. We usually had chips and soft drinks maybe some candy. Sometimes we had no tent just sleeping bags. Later we had a tent which worked better. Many times those nights would include playing hide and seek. One fateful night it had just got dark and we were playing hide and seek. All of a sudden the whole yard was lit by an eerie light. A meteorite had gone over. I believe I later read that it crashed in Canada. Steve's mother called the police and I think the local military base. I for one did not see the meteor only the ground lighting up. Those days were filled with UFO stories. Fueled by "Lost in Space" and "Star Trek" I'd guess. On more than one occasion being out at night we saw some strange things. One of the most striking was one morning when we were walking to school. We all three saw a metallic object frozen in the sky. We still all remember that. Maybe they were aware of our legendary sandlot and just wanted to come and play some sandlot ball- only got the wrong month. I know periodically at the grocery(who had a good magazine section) there would be UFO magazine or two. Of course I'd buy it. I got money for report cards which I saved. Also I also got some from grandparents or birthdays too.

I was also in the cub scouts. As a pack we had regular meetings. We pursued the different badges and I had progressed up to about Webalo level. However it was OK but I just wasn't real interested. I had tired of all that. I remember having a robot costume painted silver and made out of a box for one Halloween party. I think the similar idea was used for a knight costume as well. One time we dressed as as hula girls for a picture that was in some paper. Halloween was always fun. Gremlins would creep through the streets. I realized some costumes weren't too practical. A hard plastic mask with little eye slits was typical. I know we all got our share and more of candy… maybe a few Carmel or worse plain apples too. We quit when it became too much of a chore to carry the heavy bag.

By this time I had quite a comic book and baseball card collection. Unfortunately, before I discovered they had some value maybe around the 80s I came to the shocking/horrifying discovery they had been thrown out. By Brian's(my youngest brother) and my estimation we are talking hundreds for sure and maybe thousands. Maybe karma was at it again since some were shall we say, were ill gotten gain.

Little League ended with the Yanks in a tie for 2nd place. A couple games are mentioned in an old clipping from sports hotline. Mentioned us losing a 5-1 decision against the White Sox I pitched and lost that one. It doesn't mention a lot of details but that would have been an unexpected loss. I am surprised I pitched against them. It says I scored the only run had two hits and two walks. Then it says we came back against the Pirates to win 14-2. That game is the game I had 3 hits a single, double and HR and 3 RBIs. Two of my friends from the "C" St gang got hits against me. I guess there was no mystique for them since we played every day together on the sandlot. I think the Senators won that year. I believe we lost a close one to the Senators at the end of that season. As I mentioned we finished tied with the Pirates for second. Who won the won in the other league that year is a matter of mystery. It may have been the Mets, the Phillies or the Cardinals.

Chapter 5

School and the last year of little league"

It was soon to be the beginning of the 70s. Simon and Garfunkel had the top hit with "Bridge Over Troubled Water". I remember thinking how cool it was to sing that in music class. Other songs I especially like that year included the following: "Let It Be", "Spirit In the Sky", and "American Woman". Michael Jackson had several hits with the Jackson 5 including "I'll Be There". I also liked a singer named Melanie. Definitely a flower child type! She also had big hits like "Brand New Key" or "Look What They've done to my

Song". If you recall "Look What They've done to My Song "even had French lyrics. I even know the French part today. I even had a couple albums! Now I wish I would have used those Columbia credits for some different ones. The Partridge Family and cartoon Josie and the Pussie Cats was on TV. Music would lose some of the greats; Janis Joplin, Jim Morrison, and Jimi Hendrix. The first 747 would enter commercial service. The world wasn't getting any brighter. At least Charles Manson had been caught. May of that year had seen the horrors of Kent State. Yet more world trouble would take place with the terrorist acts at the Munich Olympics.

As was the case fall meant back to school. The Yanks title run would have to wait. We were solidly positioned for another run at the league title but an entire school year lay ahead. That was to be my last year of Little League. There was something that rang very strange about that. It just didn't seem like it should end. Some things end and new things begin. In 6th grade you moved into what used to be the high school building for Gas City. 6th grade meant you were in middle school. This old building had a couple floors. It had been the old high school in my dad's day. It was now East School and 6th through 8th graders went there. You left the newer elementary building you were familiar with where you went from 1st through 5th grade. You no longer had one teacher for every subject other than art and music. You had a home room teacher and went to specialized teachers for the various classes. A bell would ring and you had a couple minutes to change classes. I remember guys thought it was funny to knock your books out of your hand and there you would be scrambling to pick them up and make it to the next class. I remember those hallways were always packed and if they weren't you better get moving or you would be late. The book slapping thing like most mischief eventually faded out- I'm glad it did. The building had two fire escapes on the east and west side from the second floor. Funny thing I don't remember ever going down those. I had heard a kid got cut in a previous year. I remember the one on the west side had an entrance from the study hall/library on the second floor. After a period of setting empty, I believe it has now become apartments or housing of some type. The playground items like the ball fields today they have disappeared. For years the merry go round out front would go round, the swings would swing, as if invisible children were still playing. Some said it was/is haunted.

This was also the official year at least for me of discovering girls. I'm sure my daughters will enjoy this section a lot more than the previous baseball related ones. In those days, the girls would do these fancy folded notes. Some would allow for hidden messages being written on each of four folded corners. Based on some randomly picked number the count would equate to a secret message could be revealed. To my shock one time it said kiss me. Maybe they all said kiss me..hmmm. Girls were way ahead of boys then. One girl I remember would give me a note or two or three almost every day. I remember how her hand writing was really good. Handwriting compared to the generations before even that was so-so at best. Today maybe it is a completely lost art. I don't think they even practice it in school. It was risky to exchange notes in class but it happened. Some teachers would intercept and read them. Oh the horror... In my case usually it was between classes or at lunch. No recess anymore. I am not sure but maybe at least for a time she liked me! I think you as a 6th grader could attend the school dances. Regardless, I went to one and danced with my older friend's girlfriend. I remember they had some special lights even a couple lava lamps in some of the classrooms in the basement of East school. I think I danced with her on the gym floor. If I recall she was taller than I was. It was a slow dance of course. If you are aware some songs then seemed to to start slow but speeds up. Scary and awkward best describes the last minute of some. I survived. But she was very sweet. I wonder if girls realize that some guys remember that kinda thing. I guess the female phenomenon had actually started to some degree the previous year. We had a younger blonde haired music teacher who I think was a substitute. This suddenly caused all the boys to start liking music/choir a lot better.

I had one of my favorite teachers that year. I think we had our first official science class that year. We had all the usual classes as well including art and music. I still remember this brownish colored new textbook which I believe was world history of sorts. Of course part of the material dealt with the Bronze Age. I guess it was just something different than what we had up till that point. I know it covered the earliest civilizations including the Sumerians and Egyptians. I loved the illustrations in that book. Even today the History channel is among my favorites. I never thought I liked history that well but that year I did! History is riddled with mysteries. That was also the year that my baseball and education background would merge. In November of '69 we had a softball team which played the other 6th grade schools we were unbeaten. I think I homered once and maybe twice against the JC Knight team and also against the Northview team. I am not sure how many games we played but not many. Maybe it was as many as 6 or as few as 3. The guy I mentioned who was an exceptional bowler was our pitcher. Most of the others were familiar faces from little league. I remember a picture of that team. Other regulars from the sandlots and little league appear as well.

Photo from Journal Reporter

I enjoyed playing that although it was not baseball. Later, many years later, I would play many seasons on varying skill level slowpitch softball teams. I am the 2nd from the right in the front row. Sad thing about that picture is at least 2 have passed away. I enjoyed playing that although it was not baseball. I recognize my old glove in that picture. I can name many in that picture but a few I can't.

This may be jumping the gun some but above shows my final year AL champion team. I played in the all-star games again that year. I think we won both games. I pitched one of them maybe 3 inn. I hit a homerun over the scoreboard in Jonesboro in the second game. Also had a line drive single both off a lefty who I would later also homer against in the LL tournament and then again in Pony League. This was the year that my dad developed the famous ball on a string.

Basically he took a baseball and drilled about a 5/16" hole through it. I believe there was inserted a hollow aluminum piece so the cord could easily go in. Then using ¼" nylon cord he threaded the cord through the ball. Then end was secured either by flame or a knot and flame. I think I saw both eventually fail but they lasted a good while. Now even if you didn't have a lot of room or a pitcher it could be twirled from maybe 20' by almost anyone. The batter looked ahead and hit the ball as it came into view. No chasing a bunch of balls. Some guys thought it was a great aid to them! They might be right since we were scoring more runs than other teams. Besides it didn't take an expert pitcher to "throw" strikes. I guess basically it helped with the logistics I mentioned but also with developing eye hand coordination. I think it got guys used to looking ahead and picking up the ball. If the cord was not swung reasonably level it was possible to hit the cord which caused some not so nice results. Same goes for not swinging level..hitting the cord was bad.

That year toward the summer's end we as a team did candy sales. The idea was to sell enough to fund a trip up to Chicago to see the White Sox. Well the sales went pretty good but not without a hitch. I know one lady wanted to see the candy. So I attempted to open a can. Those lids were stuck very tight. The attempt ended with candy popping out and flying everywhere. The can had also flown out of my hand and landed in the grass upright. I wanted to run off... But she said- you're going to pick that up aren't you. I grabbed most and put back in. I got that can mixed up with the other ones. I ended up selling it to someone. I believe it went to my 2nd cousin. There was actually some grass in there. My teammates' dad had a large Winnebago type vehicle. I am thinking we all or most of us piled into that. I believe it was our first major league game. The game was at old Comiskey Park. The trip was icing on the cake for a good season. Using Google and finding the 1969 White Sox I'm guessing it would have been late August 16 on a Saturday. Since the White Sox were bad I doubted they won. However, it seems they did. I see they played the Yankees and surprisingly won 5-4. That may be right since I sort of recall Melton hitting a home run. Speaking of the White Sox I think that summer I wrote them and said heh you guys need to get a scout here and now. They answered back with a nice letter and said basically their scouting process would cover our area when I reach high school and keep up the good work. Last I heard from them except of course to sell me their tickets.

Concerning the losses that year, I think one was a game I was sick with stomach flu that was to the Pirates. I tried to stay in and rest. I know I had a fever most of the day. I figured I could still play. It was against the Pirates of course. No game meant more. Without going into any graphic detail I started the game pitching but somewhere in the middle I had to be taken home for shall we say a bathroom break. I came back but didn't go back into that one. That was fine with me. I had had to change the pants I had on. That was an unpleasant time to say the least.

I also think we dropped one to the Senators the first time we played. The second game was also close. In a recent conversation with my friend he recounted the last game. He was pitching with two runners on. I had pitched the previous game against the Pirates and won. He said my dad came out to the mound and gave some of that manager mound "pillow talk". He said its up to you - you can do it! The plan was brilliant. The execution was flawless. This is how it went down- he threw a wild pitch but it bounced off the back stop and then right back at our catcher who spun back to home and put the tag on the runner ending the game- Yankee's win! I know from another clipping that we played all-star game in a tournament and defeated Summitville. I was 2 for 4 with a game winning double and my teammate hit a homerun as we beat Summitville 7-6. We then lost a close one to Marion 6-5 I pitched 2 inn and gave up 2 hits and 1 run. Post season play wasn't good and wouldn't get any better.

In our local post season championship we played the Phillies. Here lies another mystery. The Cardinals only lost a single game to the Phillies. Some former Cardinals believe they won the league that year. We played the Phillies. Well you could say "played". I know we were beaten something like 12-4. I had trouble with throwing strikes and seemed to only be getting the ball across the middle of the plate.

I remember a guy stealing home when I was returning to the pitcher's mound. That wouldn't ever happen again. I was a basket case after that. I had turned my back on the runner and was walking toward the rubber. Not that many runners had been on third when I pitched. Once at the pitching rubber a runner cannot go. It ended up that guy played HS ball and several tournaments in Pony League with me in the next few years. It was a surprise to the catcher as well. When I threw he was not ready either. If there was a bright spot I homered again against that same leftie I had homered against in the all-star game. I think that was a 2 run homer. I also had another HR against him in Pony League- maybe the second longest homer I ever hit(one of those was in MSBL years later). The others on the team had some trouble with hitting this lefty. So we played bad and lost that game.

The post season was about to go from bad to worse. We drew a team from Sunnycrest league in the county tournament. Their team name was the Dragons. They featured a submarine throwing pitcher. "Knuckle-scraper" if you may. He was unlike any I had ever seen or any of us. Stuff like that messes up kids. I forget his name but believed he played HS for them later. He had a lot of strikeouts that game and that included myself. We did get one or two hits. I think one of our sandlot gang who had another year remaining was one of the few guys who got one of those hits. I again had trouble with the strike zone. Several walks compounded into what I think was about a 11-1 whomping. Not saying they didn't hit me because they did. My Little League time with the Yankees and for the 4th year guys had come to an end. You might say I flamed out. Two straight bad games is not the way you hope to go out. Maybe nerves I don't know.

After those two traumatic games I remember hitting a homerun on the sandlot..rounding the bases and thinking I was home again. We always ran out the homers..We weren't playing homerun derby. Wouldn't it be nice if after all of life's traumatic events you could just go to that safe place and forget about those bad times? Little did I realize there wouldn't be many more games at least on the little league field. For a while I had lost track of the fun in place of wanting to win worse. Quite a few root beers were bought that year. There were some highlights and good games. If I had to guess most players on our team got better. I'd guess most would vote yes to go back and relive that season again. Most had seen their first major league game. Some might have learned a little about door to door sales.

Chapter 6

After Little League- the following two years

The last chapter mentioned some of the music of 1970. '71 top hits included "Joy to the World" by Three Dog Night, and "Maggie May". I think I had all those albums. This would be the year Charles Manson would be sentenced. Millions were being executed in Cambodia. Vietnam still raged on. Top TV shows included Flip Wilson and "All in the Family".

The following years were unkind as the Yanks struggled to find replacement for the 4 departing 12 year olds. Also I think they only had one 12 year old one of the last of the sandlot guys. Today they would say it was a rebuilding year. My dad umpired in the national league that year. My middle brother played his last two years for the Yanks.

I guess LL hadn't started so great and it didn't end so great for me. Overall the middle parts were pretty awesome though. The sandlots were as fun as ever. I know we had started playing over on the Pony League diamond. The other thing to note was my brother Matt and I had had got our 10 speed bikes that prior Christmas. Mine was yellow- very cool. This meant we did bike rides around the area- mile or two in fact. The 10 speed was not the bike to try "Dead Man's hill". However it was great for riding the country roads. Riding down to the Gas City Park was almost daily. The 3 way Recreation league had started tennis lessons down there. The season ended with a tournament which I won. I got a trophy for that too. So I had two allstar trophies and a AL title trophy. They have all vanished in time. But I believe my dad's still sets on his gun case. In fact, I played the HS kid who was teaching at the end of the summer for just a set and beat him. That year I played in the county tournament and progressed to the second round. I could serve pretty well and would steadily improve over the years in tennis. A lot was going on in and around the Gas City Park. I think they had built the swimming pool and it was open at least part of that year. As much as my youngest brother Brian was there they should have named it after him. I know we would ride our bikes there. Also at the park was the old Hundley Field where I would later play high school. I remember going to watch some of the Twin City Banker games. I believe the ballpark is now named for that team. I always thought I would maybe play for them some day.

For now back to the "D" St Pony League diamond. The Pony League dugouts were real concrete enclosures. They were leftovers from a bygone era when industrial baseball ruled. In some cases good players were given regular jobs so they could play for the team. Although in 1971 there was no more teams for the local glass factories. Dugouts helped if a flash shower came thru. By this time I was often the captain. If you only had a few players, the hassle of a closed field was magnified when the left fielder would have to shift to right assuming right was normally closed. This was a lot more painful at the larger diamond. We even threw from the rubber. Curves broke more. By this time some of the older guys had moved on. We were using longer bats by that time. I don't remember many homers being hit over at the Pony League field that year. I guess center might have been around 360 ft and it was like 290-300 ft to left and right. That still kept most of our hits in the park. That is smaller than the old wooden fence which once surrounded the original field there. Bases were no longer 60 feet but now 90. That seemed like a country mile. Playing shortstop on that field was a lot more of a challenge. Generally, the same sandlot rules applied. We would still alternate some and play at the fenced LL diamond. I am not sure any of us were quite ready for the changes and challenges that lay ahead. I for one was not.

For now, let me digress and pick up some of the highlights of the 7th grade year. 7th grade was an adventure. Prior to mentioning tennis, I mentioned other sports were of course calling. I had played my first year of football for the combined East/JC Knight team. We were unbeaten and dominated all opponents. I played tackle on OL and DL. Everyone on that team probably remembers "bear walking" and "duck walking" up the hill of what is now RJ Baskett middle school. I think as a team we were in better shape than our opponents. I had made a lot of new friends from over in Jonesboro. This was the first time JC Knight and East combined for sports. Things looked bright for us in football. Each day I would ride my ten speed to the practice next to the river. My helmet and shoulder pads replaced the ball glove on the handle bars. Every day after practice on the way home I would stop at the water fountain at the local ice cream place. That would last me till I got a couple blocks to the city hall which had a better cooler water fountain. Wearing cleats I'd clippity clop into city hall to get a drink. In the winter we got to together and played tackle football in the field near the church at the end of my road. That was frowned on by coaches. Kids were hurt.

I can't skip by 7th grade so quickly without touching on gym class. Every day it seems there was a great story to tell. I will only briefly mention a few. One of our football coaches was right out of the Army I believe. Our gym classes were run "dress right dress" with the squad leader reporting on the squad's status which basically amounted to attendance of who was missing from that squad. Squad leaders would change each week. We covered most of the major sports and a lot of the minor ones in gym. I remember one time running for the entire period. I think that was about 40 minutes or so. Still up till that time it was the most I had ever done. I lasted till the end and was one of the final three or four when we were ordered back to the gym. But the game we lived for was dodge ball. It seems like the best players(throwers) managed to be on the same team(my team). That was bad news for opponents. Guys that can catch the thrown balls are also key in dodgeball . We used several of those pink dimpled inflatable balls similar to what I mentioned for kick ball. Some were slightly smaller and especially deadly. I remember usually being in the final couple guys and winning most of the time. Again this was my forte a throwing event. Even though there were bars on gym windows one time a ball busted one. I remember hearing of the following class having a full funeral for a fly when one guy in "formation" killed it. My most traumatic time came when we were playing with this 5 ft diameter ball. I will mention this later.

We also played a couple other relatively violent games. One involved a towel which was rolled up and taped. Everyone would get in a large circle holding their hands behind them. One person would drop the towel in someone's hands –that person would then chase them around attempting to hit them before they got back in the spot that was vacated. I don't remember the details but another game which I think was called spud had the loser stand leaning fwd against the wall while everyone threw volleyballs at them. You never knew what to expect in 7th grade gym.

We played a couple variations of soccer. One was called crab soccer. You walked on your hands and feet with stomach in the air like a crab. You kicked the large ball toward the opposing goal. Another version you rammed the ball or dived into it to get it across a goal line. Well one time in that game I dove as a guy stood up. The back of his head smashed me in the nose- essentially knocking me out.. although I was still remained standing. My nose was set by the teacher(I guess). You know the old fashioned two thumb squeeze method. It was broken. One nasal passage was blocked and later required surgery. The kid who unknowingly did this was a teammate on my little league team. I remember my mom coming to get me and her looking scared. I was basically OK. It looked worse than it was. It probably hurt less than after the surgery which I had at a later time. There was plenty of blood. When they take all this gauze out a couple weeks after the surgery the feeling is well..pretty mind blowing.

When spring came we were outside one time it was muddy so we all slid through the mud- very fun. I think a lot of mom's complained. Eventually softball came around. The gym teacher was all time pitcher. I remember the first day. He threw one boom- I hit it over the school. He sent me after the ball after I glowingly crossed home plate. I went around the building didn't see it. Then assumed it had bounced into the neighboring lady's rhubarb patch.. So I looked over and saw it. Of course the gate was locked but I used my fence jumping skills. I grabbed the ball and took off from behind I heard her yelling at me as I took off back to class. I think she said something about stealing her rhubarb…I got back. Truth be known I didn't like rhubarb at all. The game continued. Next time up I hit a line drive right off his shoulder. The following pitch my LL teammate put one right through the elementary window. I am not sure we played much after that. When we did some of us had to bat opposite way. We also had trampoline, wrestling, rope climbing, and gymnastics. Only time I stood on my head was in that class. I actually got 9s and 10s on stuff we did. There would not be any gymnastics medals in my future. Artist of this book was without a doubt our top gymnast.

In baseball it seemed it was back to the drawing board. Pitchers were bigger and up to age 15. Curves broke more dramatically. Even so hitting was about the same but a lot changed with respect to pitching. Wearing real spikes meant you could not slide your foot over the rubber. You had to lift it then place it against the rubber. One practice game I threw 4 straight wild pitches discovering that. My catcher saw the problem and pointed it out. In Pony League runners could lead off and steal. That meant you had to learn the nuances of the stretch and holding runners. Similar to my first year of little league the older guys who were two years ahead seemed like giants. The number of teams in Pony League was less. Some kids didn't go on to the next level. One had even died that summer of what was called "huffing". It involved spraying aerosols into a bag and breathing it. I know it was a sad time to close the door on Little League. Pony league started with a draft as well. I was taken in the second round. I know I didn't play a great amount and when I did I didn't do real well. One time though and I think it was toward the middle to end of the season I got in a game we were quite a bit ahead. I want to say it was against the Giants who were not a very strong team. I struck out 4 straight batters. I heard a guy from the dugout say "he's just throwing fastballs doesn't have a curve." Well I couldn't have that. Each of the next batter's got a curve to start. Some got it 3 straight times. Good morning, good afternoon goodnight. I had struck out 6 in a row. I also had a couple hits that game. I had some hits that season total but I'd guess my batting average was near the Mendoza line. Since we had older pitchers I didn't pitch much either. Honestly that year was somewhat a waste for me.

But there were still the sandlot games. Playing on the larger diamond became the norm. I think again growth plays a factor – I think my eyes had changed enough that was affecting my hitting. I know on the sandlots I was playing short a lot. I guess across the league many of us 13 yr olds weren't seeing a great deal of playing time. The following year my dad and another guy stepped up and said they'd take a team. I believe we were the only team added. Since my dad was the coach I went with that team although I heard my original pony league coach was not exactly thrilled with this plan. In fact, having come out of little league only a year before they were able to "cherry pick" an excellent team from those left unprotected.

The sandlot number of players had begun to dwindle. Some of the originals were now driving and rarely showed up. Although others were coming from farther distances for example the north side of town. It seems the number of games had also started to fall off. Pretty sure we were down to primarily one time a day. That meant more time to get into trouble. One of the funniest incidents I think was that summer. Our church had put in a crushed stone parking lot. Some of us neighborhood kids were there hitting rocks with an old whiffle ball bat. Well the neighbor house was only a short distance away. I believe I was the batter. After hitting several one of the rocks got by and crash…a window was broken. The "good" news was nobody was home. We immediately went over to investigate. It was the kitchen window. We couldn't see through the window that well but did see a birthday cake. It looked like glass might have gotten on that. We looked around..fortunately one of us found a dead bird.. We carefully knocked out some of the jagged glass of the remaining window. A perfect toss unto the cake and problem solved! The bird flew through the window and died on the cake..nobody eats the cake- it was brilliant. The problem though was the toss was not perfect and missed. That's when we had to get creative..one of our group said "no problem they always leave their side door unlocked". I am not sure how he knew that. Those kids were our friends though. So in we went...grabbed the bird and not only placed but pushed into the cake..and out we went. It is always best to get outta dodge in these situations. The following days were even funnier. One of the kids happened to be playing sandlot with us. He said "You guys will never believe what happened yesterday..." It was all we could do not to burst out laughing(blowing our perfect cover). He said," A bird flew through our kitchen window and died right on the birthday cake." As we took the field raucous laughter could no longer be kept in. It had to be a highlight of those days. The problem with something that great is you have to be careful who you tell. That story had the potential to go school wide. So we agreed to limit who was told. Whenever you needed a laugh it was always good to bring up. I also remember crab apple fights behind that same house. Usually it was two of us against whomever. One time though we made a mistake. We climbed into this tree house. At first it was great to throw down at the opponents. But then you run out of apples. We ambushed a group who were near the corner church softball field. We got a couple good hits in but our supplies were limited. Before long we were coated in crabapples and apple juice. When they went to find more..boom we got down and took off. Another time my neighbor finds a golf ball we sees this kid(birthday boy) climbing on the new apartment antenna tower. He says I'm going to hit him. A crab apple would have been a better choice. Wait a minute...It was a bad idea period. However, he threw it and crash a broken window resulted and this time no dead bird around. We took off but I believe he told his mother and they went over and admitted to it. Throwing things can lead to trouble. A couple years earlier one time we were having a dirt-clog fight in his back yard. I looked through a couple large branches right as one hit-funneling it into my eye. I couldn't open it but the neighbor's mother washed it out and I remember her joking about stop crying. But it was OK..but didn't seem like it at the time. I may have had some cornea scars from that. I guess it didn't matter since I would have radial keratotomy later with no problems. That following summer we were walking to the HS football games and basketball as well. Our arms again got us into trouble. During the game we had gotten a heavy wet snow. So we were walking home and near the downtown pizza joint. I think it there were 4 of us including my brother nearest my age. This is dead center Main St. Gas City. The police station is not more than a block away. Suddenly about 6 guys funnel out of the pizza place and begin to throw snowballs at us. They didn't know we were quite adept at snowball fighting. Several legendary hits against them took place. I know I hit this one kid square in the forehead. A couple of them got the idea this was a painfully bad idea. It was still great fun till one of our party threw one that busted the pizza joint's sign..that meant time to leave. I remember running across the street to the library. A few more throws ensued. But we realized the cops were coming. So we doubled back and went down allies running home. I looked back and the cops were talking to one of our foes. I could imagine how that went. I knew at least two knew me. That was a pretty heavy snow too. Only a couple chased us across the street. So ends one of the best snowball fights on record.

Trouble seemed to have a way of finding me(us). One time the street department left a skid with a detour sing and flashing lights...well we found it. We repositioned it back unto 7th street so as to detour traffic down the alley between "B" and "C" St pointing to the west. That is very narrow. I think there was one small hill there too. A couple cars fell for it and went down the alley as we hid the opposite direction toward my house and laughed. I recall a car getting stuck too but eventually it got going. A semi trailer though probably one familiar with the strange crabapple hits he would take in this neighborhood, simply crashed thru. Quickly we fetched all the pieces and reconstructed it. More fun for next hr or so this time until the cops came and took back the city's property. They even shined a flashlight toward us. We took off in a number of directions. We already had expected this eventually and had made a lot of fake paths in the snow. If I am not mistaken my buddy might have been hiding

Chris M.

inside of a bush within a few feet of the sign. That area was also the site of where we hung some type of dummy from a branch hoping a semi would hit it. I just think someone confiscated that. So in those days I don't remember having a curfew. Usually we'd be in by around 9 or 10 though.

Moving unto the following school year opened with 8th grade football. In football we were unbeaten again as 8th graders. I was the kicker that year along with playing mostly guard/tackle as I did in 7th. I made some extra pts. One against McCullough in Marion went over the fence behind the goal post. That was probably the best one I ever hit. I still have a couple clippings of some of those games. We weren't scoring as many pts that year. Seems all our opponents had grown a lot. At least that was true at the positions I played. I know the team autographed two footballs one for the case at East and one for JC Knight. I remember one at East was in a glass case of the 8th grade library. Always wondered what happened to that. Study halls were also a source of fun and mischief too. There were spit wad/paper wad fights. Some guys would make these darts and shoot them out of straws. Bulletin board tacks had a way of finding their way unto the study hall seats. But some real work got done there too. First let me say I read every paranormal book on bigfoot and ghosts they had. One of popular paranormal shows should call me to join one of his world wide paranormal investigations. They had quite a few of these books. I am guessing there were at least 15 books. I was an expert on that stuff for sure. That study hall was by far my favorite. Usually they included 7th and 6th graders as well. When I think about the study hall I remember the first time I saw a particular sweet blonde 6th grader strolling through the library. I was too chicken to even say anything to her then. I would however later meet and date her but that's another story. I am reasonably sure I did not attend any dances in 7th grade. However, in 8th I did. But they were at JC Knight. One time I went with the same guy who got me to head to the sandlot. I am certain I did not even dance with anyone. I think I talked to a couple of the football guys though. When it was over we called his brother for a ride back – well he didn't come too promptly and we started walking back. Kids there were no cell phones then so it would have been a pay phone or one in some office. Before we got too far he did show up. Another time I went with a kid from down the street. We did actually did ask a couple girls to dance. Today I wish I remembered who they were.

We also had a basketball backboard in backyard. I still have couple photos my youngest brother Brian took of me playing alone back there. He also took the best picture of me. In one I am shooting a jumper- from the angle it looks like I am like 4 feet off the ground. He later took some others which were among my all time favorites. Couldn't dribble back there so we discovered a paved court only a block away and had started playing there a lot. Little did we know the guy who owned it was a Mississinewa basketball legend and played on the real life team that was beaten by Muncie Central in the game that the movie "Hoosiers" was patterned after. We would also go down to East school and play. They had a court which kind of rivaled the sandlots in terms of guys showing up for pickup games. I wasn't much of a basketball player that is for sure. But I learned and slowly improved. In fact, I didn't make the 7th grade team but was the scorer and student manager for the team. I got to ride along to games. The team did very well. In 8th grade, though I did make the team. I could shoot but didn't really understand defenses and couldn't handle pressure well. One game though I scored 5 pts and 3 or 4 rebounds in two minutes. I think that is all I scored for the season. But practice kept me in shape. One time I got in against Justice and was supposed to foul the future Mr Indiana Basketball. He was so fast I couldn't even get close enough to foul him. A couple guys were already in foul trouble for that reason. Our team again was pretty good. One opponent had a strong player who some jokingly called the "wolfman". He did have a beard and apparently had been shaving for some time. Later I heard he was in his 3rd year of 8th grade basketball.

One last basketball related story -that is the year of the "bet". Each year the 8th grade team played the teachers. During one visit to a vending machine near the principal's office one of our top players and myself were talking to the principal. It led to us making a bet. We thought this was the year to beat the teachers. We were wrong. The 6-5 science teacher pretty much dominated the game. We lost. My friend and I were called out in front of the whole assembly. A new specially designed paddle was presented to us. We were ready to take our whack(I hadn't had one well probably since 6th and maybe 4th). We sweat bullets for a few minutes but then he let us off the hook.

Our neighborhood also had a guy who would rummage through trash cans. We called him "crowbar". I am not sure where that nickname came from exactly. I know he didn't like us calling him that and on occasion chased us. Later in an article in the local paper it was reported that he had quite a coin collection and antiques and such worth 10s of thousands of dollars. I just couldn't pass these years without mentioning him. It might have been my dad but someone also labeled him the "wolfman". We basically kept our distance but bet he was a nice enough guy. Of course there was "Wolfman Jack" and his midnight special. Also there were the classic monster movies some of which had "The Wolfman" character in it. I guess you could say "wolfman" was the most popular monster of the day. Watching scary or monster shows was another common thing on Fri or Sat night. We even liked the Abbott and Costello versions where they met Frankenstein, Mummy, Dracula, ect. The scary host that we most remember was out of Indianapolis. He was called "Sammy Terry". He would rise from a creepy casket to start the show. He wore a hood and had white make up with a fiendish laugh.

Halloween had its fun scares too. The previous year was my first for going to what was called "Scream in the Dark". This was a sort of haunted building set up by Campus Life in Marion. They spent a lot of makeup and special effects. I remember coming home from the first one and we were just up till midnight talking about it. The lines were blocks long. One year it was cold and standing in line was not very fun. Those first two years they really out did themselves. I remember that year I had been separated from my friends. I wasn't sure which way to head when out pops this glow-in-the-dark mummy. Up the stairs I go…Any horror movie affection ado would know that is bad. Once up there were several rooms. Some were dark and empty. I saw a dim light coming from the last one on the left. I headed that way… If my aging memory served me right the others were there and they gave a talk on Campus Life. I ended up being an active Campus Life member in HS and even was in 2 Scream in the Dark's my Jr and Sr year. I think "incidents" started happening with kids punching and stabbing the characters. Thus stupidity ended a pretty good thing.

Chapter 7

2nd year of Pony League for the Cardinals

Here we are up to 1972. Music in 72 remained interesting. Some of the top songs were "First Time Ever I saw your Face" by Roberta Flack, "American Pie", and "Heart of Gold". This was the year of the movie "The Godfather". "Jonathon Livingston Seagull" was a popular book. Heh these were the days of the manual kind books the ones with a cover and maybe a jacket. There were no audio books or no kindles. Bruce Lee would smash unto the movie scene amidst a wave of movies called "Kung Fu" movies. I first saw "Chinese Connection" and was an instant fan. Next was "Return of the Dragon". I was blown away. I still remember finding the Bruce Lee movies on VHS at some video store years later. I started buying Kung Fu magazines like "Black Belt". I ordered a 12 session self defense training regiment from Joe Weider. I had a strengthening device called a "bullworker". I was gaining in strength. Matt and I practiced and became quite competent with nunchakus.

As I mentioned Pony League had added at least one new team. With a brief one game exception I pretty much skipped talking about the first year of Pony League. Year two I was on the new expansion team we were the Cardinals. In fact we had a couple players who anchored the strong LL Cardinals on our team. Most of what I am going to mention was taken from some sketchy notes I scribbled down and a couple of clippings from Sports Hotline. I know we battled the Tigers that year for the title. These Tigers wore green tshirts as I remember. Other teams in the league were the Yanks, Cubs, Phillies, Red Sox, Giants, and Dodgers. It looks like I have 14 games of data not counting several practice games.

From an old Sports Hotline article I saw one game I saw I pitched a 7 inn shutout game against the Cubs allowing 4 hits and walking two. I had two hits and walked twice. Overall for the season here are my personally compiled stats. They do not count the all-star game or VFW tournament.

AB	H	2b	3b	HR	RBI	R	SAC	BOB	SO	SB	CS	BAVE
32	16	4		1	18	14	2	10	10	20	3	.500

IP	H	SO	ER	BOB	HBP	ERA(7 inn basis)	W	L
51	32	67	16	42	3	2.18	4	2

Now looking back I see that overall the numbers are solid. The homerun was one of the longest I ever hit at least until Mens Senior Baseball in 1994. It was almost dead center- was recovered across the road in the flower bed of a house there. I remember stepping it off and estimating that in the air it went around 380 feet. It was over 400 ft to where the ball was recovered. So that is one thing I have in common with the great Ted Williams. He also homered at the industrial version of that field many years earlier. He played for Grissom AFB during the time of WWII. Other surprising things that jump out at me are 20 SBs and the 42 walks- I must have always been throwing from a stretch constantly. My control was not too great -actually bad. I am sure some of the SBs were also from no throw's say when there is a runner on third and also from passed balls. Therefore that number is actually higher than an actual SB number would be. But I do know I stole some.

I also saw I played in the league all-star game. I was 2 for 5 and scored and drove in a run. In the year end tourney from my data looks like we lost in the second game. I had no hits that game. The first game which we won I was 2 for 2 with a triple(not many of those in any league). I had two RBIs and scored twice. All I showed is that I pitched and got the win.

Later that year we played for 3 way National League in the VFW tournament which was held at our field. Stats I have from that are below.

AB	H	2b	3b	HR	RBI	R	SAC	BOB	SO	SB	CS	BAVE
7	2	1	0	0	3	3	1		2	2		.285

IP	H	SO	ER	BOB	HBP	ERA(7 inn)	W	L
4 2/3	3	10	1	3		1.50	1	

We won it.

August 25, 1972 — SPORTS HOTLINE

So that year I think I was voted our team MVP. I got a trophy for that. Also I received the one for the VFW tournament win. I don't recall if there was one for the all-star game or not. All of these trophies along with several others didn't make one of my moves… darn it. But at the time the order of the universe was restored I was back near the top of the ball diamond again.

That was also the summer going into freshman year. All incoming freshman had to walk on pins and needles for fear of "initiation". The most common form of this was being made to push a penny with the nose for a couple feet. It would often leave a skinned spot on the nose for a week or two. Few avoided it. Usually odds are stacked against you like two upper classmen and you. Or 3 or 4 upper classmen vs 2 freshmen was also typical. I didn't hear much about the case when of one upper classman alone "initiated" an incoming freshman. It happened to me(and my buddy) late that summer while walking with one of my football friends—just outside of east school . Also would happen again near the football field. After that I was done..next time was going to mean a fight.

My notes seem to indicate that I missed two games that year. I believe that is the year we went to Fl. We went that year to Florida with my parents. I don't remember a whole lot about that trip. There are quite a few pictures from places like Silver Springs and others. But high school was around the corner. A whole assortment of new adventures came with that.

Chapter 8

The last year of Pony League

1973 had come and summer with it. This year top songs included "Bad Leroy Brown", "Killing Me Softly with His Song", "Crocodile Rock", "Seasons in The Sun", and "You're So Vain" to name a few. Watergate was breaking or should I say being broken into, or maybe leaking is the right word. The Wooded Knee Massacre happened. With little or no fanfare my high school years had begun.

In the late summer HS freshman football was well underway. I remember being late for class and hearing the Vice principal holler at me- "Come here boy". I said "but, I'm late for class". He said..." That's OK, what's your name?" I told him. "He said, "you any relation to Bob M(my dad)?" I said yes "He's my dad." He smiled and said "Yes, now we are going to have a ball team again!" I went on to class late. At the time I didn't realize he had been my dad's coach. In football we remained undefeated until losing a close one to nearby county school. Some very suspicious calls took place in that game. We heard the referee's had nephews and even a son playing for our opponent in that game. We lost 14-12. Regardless of the loss that year was a lot of fun. We won 6 games including beating Marion.

One incident that I remember went down like this. I often walked across the street to eat lunch at Dairy Queen. On this particular day our high school made national news by staging a walkout. I think primarily upper classmen were involved in it. Part of the issue involved 2/3 guys being told to get a haircut. Their response was not to get a haircut but rather get a lawyer. Somehow this blew back on the principal who was dismissed. I remember a reporter and a guy with a camera coming up to me and asking "Are you part of the walk out". I answered no "I'm at lunch" and he quickly found someone else. I remember returning to class and majority of people(freshmen) were there. Teachers didn't really know what to do. As I remember it had to do with school board firing the principal. So the civil unrest had even filtered down to small town schools I guess. It was a time that racial troubles were taking place in Marion. I heard many say they had a shotgun in the trunk of their car. It seems like I recall an incident involving students from nearby school showing up and fighting with some of our students in the parking lot. One of our top football players was involved.

After being the last guy cut from the freshman basketball team I went out for wrestling. I didn't have much experience and freshman for the most part didn't have a lot of times to actually wrestle. I got pinned in the open house meet. But I slowly improved after that. I was ahead in a freshman wrestling tournament weighing 165 wrestling at 185 against the guy who won it. I was ahead 13-3 going into the final period. However one error and I got pinned. I was 1-1-1 in B-team matches. One time against nearby school varsity and our 167 lb guy had not made weight. Three of us were running trying to make weight. I lost a couple pounds but didn't quite get there. That was probably a good thing. The opponent was a regional champ and easily pinned the guy who did make weight in record time. I not only made the chess club but was voted the president the following year.

Spring came and it was baseball time. I had gone out for the varsity team. I remember putting some good practices together. It seems like a lot of guys had gone out that year. In fact I tended to do well in practice. I remember seeing 4 of us freshmen had made the team! I played enough to get a varsity letter. I had a couple of wins as a

Chris M.

pitcher. I remember having a couple multiple hit games also. I was playing left field and pitching for the most part. I have some clipping from the paper on some of those games. However, I am just going to touch on a few highlights. Grant County had some excellent teams that year. By my notes we were 20-11. We had a good varsity team but lost in the first game of the sectional. We also had a few B-team games a handful of games. I had strong games in all with several hits and throwing out a couple runners from left. I also pitched in one of those games. That year we also played an unofficial area HS team that year. We won I think 12-0. I split pitching duties and left with 6 K's in 4 inn. Also I had a couple hits including a double off the fence. At the end of the game I heard one of the players say that game didn't count for stats. Really, it didn't matter to me I played all games the same. They all counted in my book. That year I played in the 4 B-team games and about 10 or so Varsity games. Coaches worked together with respect to my pitching so I didn't throw too much. Also at that time my last year of Pony League was going on. Sometimes I would leave one game and head straight to Hundley for another or even two more! Those were fun times.

I did keep some accurate notes on the Pony League games that year. That year in Pony League we won both the league and the tournament. It was overall my best year in any 3-Way league. Due to pitching issues involving HS and B-team I pitched less than the previous year. According to my notes I don't see that we lost a game. Many games I would throw 4/5 innings with someone else coming in to close or vise versa.

AB	H	2b	3b	HR	RBI	R	SAC	BOB	SO	SB	CS	BAVE
39	29	4	3	1	25	22	4	8	2	X	X	.743

IP	H	SO	ER	BOB	HBP	ERA(7 inn)	W	L	Save
34	15	58	8	29	3	1.64	5	0	2

From my notes and an old clipping the season went like this:

Cards 7 Giants 6

Cards 20 Dodgers 3

Cards 8 Tigers 3

Cards 15 Phillies 2 (I was 4-4 with a double and pitched 5 inn SO 8 and W)

Cards 2 Yanks 1

Cards 11 Red Sox 3 (pitched 6 inn So 12 and got the win)

I also played in the Allstar game that year. The game was at Hundley field. I had one hit, a sac fly, scored 1 run and pitched one uneventful inn. That game our SS took a ball off the forehead when it came unexpectedly up off the edge of the grass. It wasn't a pretty sight from any angle. But I had a birds eye view since I was the third baseman next to the play. You see our Pony league field did not have grass. I did not record the outcome of that game. I am pretty sure our team lost.

The second half went like this

Cards 6 Dodgers 3

Cards 10 Cubs 1

Cards 9 Giants 1 (I was 2 for 4 with a triple, pitched 7 inn had 11 Ks, my friend reminded me of a double he hit to break up a no-hitter)

Cards 8 Tigers 4

Cards 21 Red Sox 4(I was 3 for 4 pitched 3 inn had 7 ks)

Cards 16 Phillies 2

Cards 13 Yanks 3

Chris M.

Tournament (Very sketchy reading my old faded chicken scratches and old clippings)

Cards 6 Cubs 4

Cards 10 Dodgers 9

In that year's VFW tournament according to Sport's Hotline we beat Summitville 7-0 and Gas City American 8-7. I pitched 4 inn of the Summitville game as a teammate and I combined on a 1 hitter. I had a double and two singles w a couple RBI's in that game. I only had one hit w a couple walks and scored twice. My records show us losing to Gas City American 10-6 so I am not sure what is going on with respect to this. Just don't remember. I am pretty sure I did not have two VFW tournament trophies so I suspect I am right.

The thing I remember the most about that season wasn't so much the winning but it was playing quite a few more games than I was used to. The league was composed of a great bunch of guys. It was the most fun season of baseball I ever had. Another thing that sticks out is I played a fair amount of first base in Pony League that year. Our main pitcher who won our MVP that year had a good pickoff move. I saw in the clipping he won the first three games that year. He put together some great games at the plate as well. Pitching though I swear he would walk guys sometimes just to pick them off. I know we picked off two Tigers in one inning and one was another freshman playing varsity with me. I bet he picked off a dozen guys. From my notes it looks like we won every game. That last year I had my highest batting average ever. I guess if I could relive one year of baseball this would be it.

I am fairly certain my sandlot times and quite probably most of those remaining in that area were winding down. I don't think there were enough kids of that age range coming up. Those that were had other interests. That last summer with varsity and b team games as well as the regular Pony League games there was less time to play sandlot ball. I wonder now what my last time playing sandlot ball actually was like. Many of you probably wonder why I would even care. My answer would be I guess you had to live it. I am sure I found my way there a few more times though. I know years later when the fences came down it troubled me. The field though became filled with weeds and remained for years. Slowly one by one houses began a relentless march across the fields where the sandlots once stood. And now the march is complete. No backstops, no lights, and no fields remain. Only the fading memories in the minds of those that grew up and lived near there remain. As far as I know I think 5 of the sandlot kids played in HS. One teammate from the Cardinals played one HS game. A few of us(Little League and sandlot) played in other leagues through college and even in Men's leagues. Many including myself also played on slow pitch teams in that and other areas. I played some form of organized ball every year from 1967 till 2002. Then I played again in 2005 and 2006. That's 35 years plus 2. That is a lot of bat swings, balls caught, and balls thrown. Many coached their own children through a variety of sports. Baseball movies definitely caught some of the spirit of the sandlot game. While none of us went to the majors and played. Most all of us enjoyed the game to some degree if only just to watch. I bet most remember that first hit or the time they got picked first. I have talked to several of those players from those old teams. Almost all I see a smile as I listen to a favorite memory being recounted. I probably have forgotten much more than I have managed to put into these pages. While centered around my baseball days hopefully people can see a bit of a snapshot of how life as a kid in a small town was. I have mentioned thanking people. First I dedicate this to my dad who introduced me and diligently trained me in the finer arts of this game. Next I am thankful to all those teammates from organized ball. I am also thankful to all those who spent those hot dusty mornings and afternoons on the sandlot. Finally, I am thankful to God for a chance to recount these days. Who knows maybe somewhere in the sky is one more game. I mentioned looking back on the picture of our 3 Way Pony League team and noting one of those has already passed on.

I guess eventually just like the way the houses moved across the fields. Life takes over the ball playing time. Work, school, marriage and many things become the priorities as they should. I wish kids everywhere could at least have experienced some thrills and spills that can be had playing on the sandlots. Even if perfectly groomed fields sat open all day long I doubt they would attract few if any players. Video games have become a past time now. They can be played in air conditioned homes. They probably end up costing a lot more than a bat, a ball and a glove. I am not sure how many of today's serious players get burnt out or injured by playing too much with the practice and travel ball. Today too there are so many other things competing for players. Soccer has grown. Today finding spare property where a field could be built could be a challenge as well. Today many communities are just to unsafe to have young kids out alone. I remember a couple years ago stopped at a light in Yuma watching a dust devil travel through an empty field. Then by the time the light turned it was gone. I remember thinking how quickly these glory days came and went. Fields are gone..only a few fading memories remain. I hope if some of that old gang and others my age read this they are able to remember a few of these. Hope some of the stories cracked a smile or two. If you are a youngster I hope you find some place you can give this a try. Recently, I heard the new commissioner of baseball is concerned that this generation is not so plugged into the game. Who knows what 10 years will bring. I have lived long enough to know that sometimes what goes around comes along. Maybe one day in small towns surrounded by cornfields new ball fields will spring up and new tales of fun in the sun will arise.

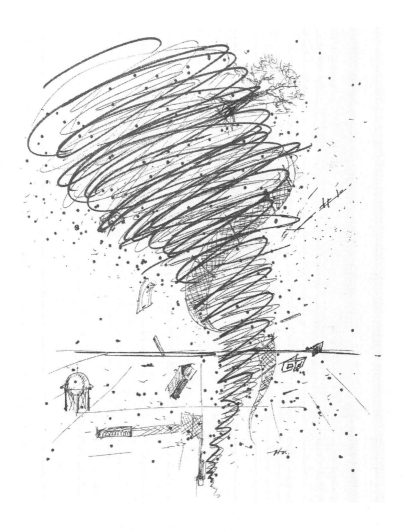

Made in the USA
Lexington, KY
26 October 2016